JOSÉ ESTEBAN ORIA

WHEN FLEEING VENEZUELA BECOMES A QUESTION OF LIFE OR DEATH

SUMMONS, ARRESTS, TORTURE, FORCED DISAPPEARANCES, AND EXTRAJUDICIAL EXECUTIONS UNDER THE TYRANNY OF MADURO

IT IS A BOOK OF LIVED EXPERIENCES

José Esteban Oria

DEDICATION

This book is dedicated to the memory of the beloved brother's Oscar Pérez and José Pimentel, members of the respectable lodge Santiago Mariño Number 208. Their fight for the freedom of Venezuela continues in force.

CONTENTS

ACKNOWLEDGEMENTS

Writing this work is closing a cycle and probably opening another. It is to order a passage of my life and leave a testimony of my recent history.

None of this would have been possible without the brave stories of my brothers. I know what this has meant for them, to relive those moments, often stormy, nightmares, and anguish, because sometimes we want to move on; however, there are people behind who need an answer, and that is what we have done.

I am eternally grateful to Ángel Fajardo, a fantastic older man who picked up the phone and called me from France to give me the best news. The international protection system recognized him as a legitimate victim of a process of systematic human rights violations against Freemasons carried out by the Maduro regime and his collaborators. He vindicated our work and our complaints.

Thanks to the asylum case of Ángel Fajardo, the first jurisprudence was created that recognizes a Freemason, particularly a member of the Santiago Mariño Lodge Number 208, as an indirect victim who suffered damage as a result of the injury sustained by the victim Direct, in this case, his lodge brothers Oscar Pérez and José Pimentel, setting a precedent and legal basis to defend other Freemasons in the same condition; he is also the first citizen of Venezuela to be given protection for his status as a Freemason.

I want to thank William Jiménez, a brother with more than 20 years of friendship. William is a public relations man, a generous and helpful being, and very outgoing. I remember our gatherings in Caracas, and we were always planning the return of democracy.

William risked denouncing irregularities of which he was a witness; he exposed the chain of command present during the autopsy of Oscar Pérez, a fact that has led him to be summoned as a witness before the

International Criminal Court. William was a visiting member of the Santiago Mariño N 208 lodge; he has been a bulwark in defense of the Freemasons.

William received political asylum from the kingdom of Holland; he became the second Freemason to have protection for the cause related to the case of brother Oscar Pérez. William Jiménez has been a fraternal brother whom I have counted on to expose the whole truth and take our complaints to the International Criminal Court.

A very special thank you to Endry Méndez; I know how difficult these years of exile have been for him, suffering from injuries caused by an alleged attack against him while he was working. Endry is a former scientific police investigator who has denounced forced disappearances of Freemasons and has exposed a truth that they tried to hide from the highest hierarchies of power in Venezuela and the Grand Lodge.

Writing a book about your life story is a surreal process. I will always be indebted to the life that has allowed me to tell it.

Finally, thanks to all those who have been part of my path.

A STORY TO TELL

Today, March 5, 2023, I sent the International Criminal Court my completed form to consult the opinions and observations of the victims on resuming the investigation in the Situation of Venezuela I, I did not want the detail to escape me, for that reason, I have finished this book on time, which serves as a backup for all the information sent. I didn't keep anything, and the whole story is contained in these line.

PROLOGUE

Introduction
"If you are neutral in situations of injustice, you have chosen the oppressor's side."
Desmond Tutu

Despite the harsh circumstances in which all Venezuelans were, I refused to leave Venezuela; an unexpected event made me change my mind; there was so much uncertainty and threat that I opted for an unplanned departure and abrupt departure from Venezuela to the United States.

My work offers a fundamental description of what is happening in Venezuela; it is a document that captures a stage of my life in which I witnessed actual events, which can even be considered documents of interest for analysis in rights. Human rights, to clarify the behavior of some relevant actors in the Venezuelan political and military scene to strengthen the causes of justice in the competent courts, in particular, I have taken the time to write about the persecution that was done to Freemasons, in the framework of the search that the Maduro regime deployed against Oscar Pérez, a fact that directly affected me.

This inhumane act committed by the regime against Oscar Pérez and his group, which ended up taking their lives through extrajudicial executions, affected many people directly or indirectly related to Oscar, but perhaps one of the least known and most impactful aspects was the way a systematic violation of human rights against members of the Freemason community, of which we were members together with Oscar Pérez. We will read about this and more in my work.

INTRODUCTION

ESCAPING FROM A BIG JAIL CALLED VENEZUELA

I think that the military counterintelligence of Nicolas Maduro is the main source and source of the strategy of political and social control in Venezuela.

They are known as the DGCIM General Directorate of Military Counterintelligence, and they share support tasks for the operation of the Maduro regime with their partners in the SEBIN Bolivarian Intelligence Service and the CICPC Scientific, Criminal, and Criminal Investigation Corps.

Some of his domination strategies, from his office's infiltration actions, are planned and carried out in organizations such as unions, universities, unions, churches, and lodges to recruit collaborators, carry out intelligence, and collect and collect and update data.

These highly specialized officials in social control can create fictitious scenarios to entertain and divert the attention of millions of citizens, as they have been doing for more than 20 years since they took power in Venezuela.

Helped by the Cubans and Russians, these agencies have become expert propagandists, creators of stories to play with the minds of the people they keep in permanent anxiety. They are the ones who help the regime's economists by bringing chaos. In contrast, the others trigger inflation by printing inorganic money with the objective that people spend their life looking for food, medicine, and gasoline, navigating scarcity and misery. , that is the way Maduro sustains himself.

These agencies really rule Venezuela with a heavy hand; they are in charge of silencing the critics, those who protest.

From Miraflores, they work inventing false enemies, facing each other, and dividing society, friendships, and families.

The domination model is fundamentally based on data manipulation on an individual and global scale. So to function in Venezuela, the telephone companies have to allow access to the state; With this technology at its disposal, the Maduro regime sees, hears, and records everything. They use the press and social networks, which they control at will since, in Venezuela, there is only one internet and telephone provider, the CANTV company, because the rest of the private providers have a license that is monitored by the state through CONATEL, which has full control capacity; of intervention.

Movistar admits that by Maduro government orders, it intercepts communications from 20% of its customers.

These Venezuelan state agencies, read DGCIM, SEBIN, and CICPC, are responsible for disseminating false messages. The immediate goal is to focus the public's attention on the regime's lies and keep them from raising awareness and reflecting on the serious problems that afflict. In this way, the Venezuelan people live in a bubble, entertained by Maduro's scene montages; among Maduro's recurring stories are the assassinations against Maduro, lies where many innocent people are implicated, where there are arrests, torture, injuries, and deaths.

Publication in INFOBAE denounces that the DGCIM, SEBIN, and the CICPC are the Venezuelan state agencies with the highest number of tortures and arbitrary detentions in Venezuela.

These officials can use public and private media and social network influencers who are paid salaries in dollars; they also have agents deployed in all sectors of social life with the idea of infiltrating to obtain sensitive information from politicians. , people of art, journalists, influencers, media editors, opinion columnists, and public figures.

They can manipulate any form of fact or circumstance to produce incriminating legal documents, using their branches in the Judicial System, including officials from the Supreme Court of Justice, the Prosecutor's Office, and the Courts.

Publication in @elpitazo denounces that DGCIM is looking for possible allies of Oscar Pérez in Masonic lodges.

Its actions include planting evidence, creating files, manipulating data, extorting victims' relatives, making arbitrary arrests, torture, forced disappearances, and extrajudicial executions. Its main commandos answer directly to the office of the Maduro Presidency. Therefore, they have sufficient funds and unlimited money from the direct coffers of Maduro; all the dollars and petrodollars are at their disposal because they are the ones who keep Maduro in power; They know the smallest detail of the life of the opponents, their private lives, their assets, everything is served so that they are extorted and blackmailed by these agents.

There is no doubt about how sinister these Maduro military and police agencies are. In all social circles, they have collaborators for their intelligence, create and delete evidence, and have a way of disappearing or creating stories for you. To mention one of the matters of greatest interest and importance is the statistics on arbitrary arrests and disappearances; human rights organizations in the UN hold these organizations responsible for more than 2,000 cases of forced disappearances in Venezuela; they have machinery efficient, which has a social and corporate fabric in which many people participate.

Suppose you are suspected of being on the radar of some of the agencies as mentioned earlier for some political reason, even if the cause is non-binding or you are not responsible, call yourself SEBIN, DGCIM, or CICPC; this can mean anything from harassment, harassment, threats, or arrest without a warrant, torture, and disappearances. They come against their closest relatives, wife, children, or parents if they do not find who they are looking for. For that reason, it is called the terror machine.

Logic indicates that before being brought before one of these agencies, it is best to go into hiding or exile; You don't play with these people.

When it comes to DGCIM, SEBIN, or CICPC, you have to consider what type of danger one may be involved in or involuntarily involved in; I am going to tell you about my case, which is the reason why I wrote this book, on occasion Oscar Pérez's connection with my lodge, the CICPC and DGCIM agents were present in my lodge, over some time a series of events took place, summonses, arrests, torture, and disappearances.

I decided to leave Venezuela as soon as I found out about the summons to some lodge members. In the end, the facts proved me right, as long as I made the correct decision to leave the country, before the rest of the chain of events ended in our lodge, due to the act of constitutional rebellion of the freemason Oscar Pérez, I say constitutionally given account his disobedience was argued under the precept established in article 350 of the constitution of Venezuela.

WHAT WE WILL READ IN MY WORK

The work essentially deals with narrating episodes of my life in which I saw irrefutable acts of human rights violations by the Venezuelan state. I recount my experience as a witness of the attacks by the Maduro collectives on the office of the Venezuelan Federation of Political

Scientists in the El Nacional building in El Silencio, also the siege of the national parliament, and finally, the persecution of Freemasons in the framework of the hunt that did the Maduro regime against Oscar Pérez.

This is a personal analysis given that I experienced it firsthand, the specific case of Oscar Pérez, I dedicated enough time to explain it because he was an active member of my lodge Santiago Mariño Number 208, and for this reason, the Maduro regime initiated an intervention in Freemasonry that began as a search and led to a brutal hunt for Freemasons that resulted in arrest, torture, executions, alleged forced disappearances, exiles and attacks abroad.

I have addressed all these aspects in this book, providing details that help to understand the events. I remember that three years after the Junquito massacre, I found out that a member of the lodge had been arrested in July 2017, two weeks after the Oscar uprising; he was presented before a military court; in his statement, you can read that I mention Freemasonry at least three times, which can be interpreted as an alleged implication of the order, I address this passage in more depth in the interior body of my work.

Another aspect of interest addressed in my book is the alleged collaboration of some Freemasonry authorities of that time with the Maduro regime. I will relate the topics that led me to this conclusion.

It is important to note that all these complaints have been investigated throughout these four years, from the fateful events of the Junquito massacre, where Oscar Pérez and his group were murdered. I have made them public in my opinion column in the influential newspaper El Nacional; the result is that today they are the subject of an investigation by international organizations.

I have denounced the alleged collaboration of a small group of Freemasons with Maduro to the detriment of dissident Freemasons of the regime because it is necessary to show the audience the differences between the Freemasons in Venezuela.

Publication in El Cooperante denounces that DGCIM raided Masonic lodges in 6 states looking for possible allies of Oscar Pérez.

Because the complaint about the persecution of the Freemasons made by the Maduro regime was public and notorious by the press, the International Criminal Court or the competent court will probably conduct an investigation and call the victims and witnesses, so The publications of the complaints are intended to assist the investigators, so that they do not confuse the victims, the witnesses with alleged collaborators or perpetrators, and in particular I emphasize the performance of the Past Grand Master, Colonel Jiménez Silva and other actors of the board of the year 2018, of whom I have requested be investigated by the law.

It is important to note that I have sent public letters to Prosecutor Karim Khan of the International Criminal Court, which has been answered, emphasizing continuing the investigation of these alleged crimes against the Freemasons Oscar Pérez and José Pimentel and their companions, considered crimes against humanity.

Recently, we have learned of other alleged state crimes against Freemasons, which, according to an investigator, are related to the Oscar Pérez case: The names Wilmer Muñoz and Juan Hurtado, both presumed forcibly disappeared, have also been mentioned in these cases and requested an investigation before the ICC.

My book follows a chain of events that may show that the Venezuelan state is involved and systematically acted criminally against Freemasons, motivated by their claim to capture Oscar Pérez.

My account covers what I know about the arrests, tortures, disappearances, and Masons fleeing due to this persecution of Maduro, which gives a new meaning to the persecution of Masons in Venezuela.

The most visible consequence is the international recognition of the international refuge for Venezuelan Freemasons, in the case of granting the first political asylum granted by a French court under the argument of the danger to the life of the Freemason Ángel Fajardo due to his membership in the same lodge. The opponent Oscar Pérez attended, legal evidence that this lodge followed by Oscar Pérez is an indirect victim of human rights violations by the Maduro regime.

This book is an invaluable document that can help understand why Venezuelans are fleeing Maduro and should be protected by the states.

Esteban Oria writing his book

OPINION COLUMNIST WHO IS NOT AFRAID, TO TELL THE TRUTH

Esteban Oria, director of the organizing committee for technology events with a massive presence of attendees.

I remember that in 2014 I had already warned about Maduro's political temperament; I wrote one of my most challenging posts for that moment, entitled "He doesn't look like Chávez," published on the previous El Nacional web platform. Currently, I was able to get it. Published in the digital version of the newspaper El Mercurio de Chile. What I essentially said in that post was that Maduro was going to become something worse than Chávez, I am going to share a summary made by the Caracol Radio portal about my post, and he quotes: "it points out the profound differences between the governments of the late Hugo Chávez and his successor, warning that factors such as repression, lack of leadership and the falling economy have made the government of Nicolás Maduro disastrous." El Nacional: It doesn't look like Chávez because of Esteban Oria."

Writing has always been my passion; I did it from a very young age; my first articles were for a light column that I got in Dominical magazine, a publication that appeared in the Ultimas Noticias newspaper. At that time, its director was Hortensia Bracamonte, and the newspaper's owner was the famous Don Miguel Ángel Capriles Ayala.

In Dominical magazine, my posts were essentially about tourism and general culture. I remember a friend lent me his old Zenith camera; I used it frequently at work. I was encouraged to tour Venezuela because I could communicate with so many people. In each town I visited, I wrote the stories of it; I took photos of the historical sites, the cathedrals and churches, and the government palaces particularly caught my attention; those were my first steps in opinion writing.

Later my first articles on politics appeared in the newspaper La religión; it was an opportunity that General Ennio Torres gave me; he was director-editor of this prestigious Catholic newspaper. I titled my column "Letters to Chávez" because it addressed topics that dealt with certain issues of his administration, so I wrote my criticisms of him ironically.

The newspaper did not have a large circulation; its importance lay in the printer; it was the official newspaper of the Catholic Church, which was printed right in front of the civil powers that Chávez controlled, such as the governor's office and the mayor's office of Caracas.

I always knew that these chavismo people were dangerous; the only armor I had was my ability to be diplomatic enough to tell some truths without making them uncomfortable. So writing about politics during that time with a hegemonic Chávez as an opponent meant a great challenge; I learned to be critical of Chávez seeking to qualify my denunciations, trying to be acceptable by the standards of tolerance in his government.

WRITING IN THE NATIONAL

After a period of literary pause, and during a Dudamel concert at the Teresa Carreño, I had the honor of meeting Dr. Miguel Henrique Otero; I remember that on that occasion, I introduced myself as president of the Venezuelan Federation of Political Scientists for true, an organization that we had created a group of political scientists from different universities and political parties.

From the beginning, we received his support, and he was and continues to be a first-rate public figure in Venezuela. We invite you to our first day of political science held in a hotel room in Chacao; the event brought together hundreds of political scientists from all over Venezuela, in addition to the presence of Dr. Henrique Otero, the vice minister of CORDIPLAN, the political scientist Miguel Van Der Dij, who was a professor at our School of Political Studies at the Central University of Venezuela, the Costa Rican ambassador to Venezuela Vladimir de la Cruz and other prominent personalities.

Over time, these activities gave rise to events for political scientists in the El Nacional auditorium at its headquarters in Los Cortijos. The open government forum was one of the events that brought together the largest number of political scientists and people linked to the sector. Then the activities of the political scientists continued in said auditorium with the accompaniment of El Nacional. The events allowed us to maintain a permanent union activity..

Esteban Oria welcomes the attendees to the Conference on Political Science in 2010

At that time, Chavismo dominated all spheres of power. It wasn't straightforward for political scientists unrelated to Chávez to get a job because I had signed the Tascón list or the recall.

To make a little history, those of us who signed to revoke Chávez's mandate in 2004 were included by Jorge Rodríguez in the Tascón list. Jorge is the current president of the illegitimate National Assembly, who at that time was the director of the National Electoral Council. To prevent Chávez from being revoked, Rodríguez included more than 3 million signatories in a list that he circulated in the offices and ministries called the Tascón list, with the objective that it be crossed with the human resources database, and the order was to dismiss to those who were found or rejected job applications.

In this way, millions of citizens were fired from their jobs; I denounced this crime at its opportunity, participating in the creation of the committee of victims of the Tascón list.

I remember when I was banned from working for the State, which was my primary source of employment as a political scientist, I was forced to learn a new trade and thus migrated to the technological field.

Self-taught, I learned to design web pages and multimedia presentations, then I assimilated the art of video and photography editing. Over time, in addition to providing services, I began to organize technological events; I ended up holding high-impact fairs, congresses, and seminars in Caracas.

My foundation called, Propymettic, received the support of most of the critical technology corporations; we offered speaker seats to exhibitors of international stature, about this there is a lot of information consulting YouTube with the criteria of words "Internet Caracas 2011 ", "National Congress of Web and Mobile Technology, UCV," "Expotic from the years 2014 – 2016 Venezuela" and "Android Meeting 2014 and 2016".

The organization of events did not prevent me from doing my job as a political communicator, so on one occasion, Doctor Miguel Henrique invited me to write as a columnist for his newspaper; it meant one of the greatest honors received; I immediately accepted it without reservation, aware of the implicit meaning of writing in a symbolic newspaper of Venezuelan democracy, at a time when the Chávez government was becoming more and more sinister, and dangerous.

During that time, I also had the distinction of receiving the academic endorsement of the Central University to dictate my Digital Marketing and Social Media diplomas; they were very fruitful moments in which I gave all my knowledge and put it at the service of Venezuelan education until then. I felt like part of a Venezuela that refused to die before the boot of tyranny; We are talking about the years 2012 and 2016.

Images of Esteban Oria with his students from the Digital Marketing graduates at the Central University of Venezuela and the El Nacional facilities and during his graduation in the marketing specialization.

During the period I graduated, we could train more than 1000 students between attendees to the face-to-face and online modes. Undoubtedly, both the Central University of Venezuela and the newspaper El Nacional were my fundamental allies in this work of dissemination and academic training. I will always be grateful to them.

VENEZUELAN FEDERATION OF POLITICAL EXPERTS, WITNESS TO THE ASSAULT ON THE PRESS

José Esteban Oria during the opening of the Electronic Government forum in the El Nacional auditorium at the Los Cortijos headquarters

In my tenure as president of the Venezuelan Federation of Political Scientists, known by the acronym Fedepolitologos, together with my colleagues on the board, during the Chávez era, we tried to promote a peaceful solution to the political crisis, we organized events to warn about the danger of losing democracy in Venezuela.

The response we got from the regime was contempt for the debate of ideas and constant siege. In previous paragraphs, I told you we were attacked while leaving the Federation offices by these savage and violent groups known as "colectivos." During the attacks against colleague Freddy Torres, he was beaten and tortured by security organizations. of Maduro.

Freddy had to leave Venezuela. Initially, he traveled from Colombia to Panama, thanks to the support of an essential former senator from Copey, who asked the popular party for help. It was in this way that Freddy managed to land in Spain.

Freddy Torres is one of the bravest people I have ever met, and he died in exile after he arrived in Spain, a death that shocked us. He was afflicted with diseases caused by the martyrdom he suffered in Venezuela due to the persecutions and abuses committed by his.

Freddy Torres, politically persecuted vice president of the Venezuelan Federation of Political Scientists, dies in exile in Spain.

These are diseases generated by the high psychological stress produced by the Maduro police state to which he was exposed, inducing anxieties and ailments resulting in traumas and heart problems of incalculable consequences.

Like Freddy, I also lived under Maduro's stalking; in my particular case, I could occasionally observe the presence of cars with smoked windows in front of the building where we lived.

I remember that my cell phone was practically useless due to the excessive echo in the earpiece, which occurred when I received or made calls.

It was a nightmare to communicate with me; you had to guess what the interlocutor was saying practically; the echo sometimes mixed with the next echo, and the monitoring caused all these communication problems that the political police do when tapping the phones.

Despite these harsh circumstances and the fear that living under the shadow of state surveillance generated, I always maintained hope for a peaceful change, I was always involved in political activities, supporting electoral initiatives seeking to participate, pushing and proposing solutions, so I never stopped to attend the invitations that the press and television sent me, aware of the enormous risk that this entailed..

Esteban Oria guests in prestigious TV shows

I remember that before being interviewed, I prepared myself mentally to measure each word that I was going to say to avoid being the object of direct reprisals from the political police, so I practically had a script where I focused my conversations on electoral issues, relationships international and academic, but avoided making references to some specific and controversial issues of the Chávez family since being in Venezuela meant a direct ticket to jail. Some of my videos can be found on YouTube with the criteria of words "Esteban Oria Globovision.".

MY EXPERIENCE WITH CUBAN INTELLIGENCE

I want to make a parenthesis in this chapter to tell you about a fact that happened to me with the issue of state surveillance; on this topic, I wrote a post with a complete reference in my opinion column for El Nacional under the title "Telephone espionage and cybernetic in the Venezuela of Maduro," I am going to share an extract of the content of my reading:

"This is the sad reality of Venezuela in the hands of Maduro, turned into a gigantic cyber prison. In one of my posts, I told you about my experience with a Cuban doctor. It happens that I visited her in a CDI. When I got home, I turned on the computer, and, surprise, I had an additional email in my email inbox in my Gmail that brought a password. When I clicked on it, the session opened, and who was in the photo in the email was precisely this Cuban doctor; that is what this issue of electronic espionage is about; I believe it is true; it cannot be denied that it has worked for Maduro. He knows many people's lives, and to some extent, this can explain the behavior of some opposition actors; the truth is that they listen to you, and the best advice we can give is while you are in that jail, say what they want to hear."

So it was in this way that I discovered that I was also being monitored at a cyber level; I asked myself the question, how is it possible that Gmail, in the field where I put the emails, appears a drop-down list with an unknown email address, that it also comes with a password, that when I clicked on it, I could log in and see all the content of that email? The owner was one of the doctors who had checked me days before at the CDI, and I found out when I saw her profile picture in the mail.

I am not a cybersecurity expert, and I will not give conclusions on this, nor the way or the tools they used, but this confirmed to me the espionage issue of Cuban doctors; not all of them come to treat patients in Venezuela, some honor their oath Hippocratic, but others are part of the sinister intelligence network at the service of Maduro.

So the espionage situation was a critical issue; I was aware of this danger, I took care of everything I said or spoke inside my home, but above all, I always expressed what I wanted others to hear. The same thing happened with the telephone; I had already mentioned that it was practically impossible to converse with people due to the difficulties of mixing with the echo. In the end, living that way was frankly miserable; that's what the Maduro dictatorship is about, and that was why people fought in the streets against the regime during the demonstrations in 2017; we know that we live in prison.

If we temporarily locate ourselves in time, we are talking about a cycle of my life that covered from 2014 to 2017; it was a very turbulent period marked by anti-government protests that left a balance of victims of more than 200 people. In this charged environment of violence, with Maduro using the state's power to assassinate opponents, I was trying to have a life during the chaos.

THE ASSAULT ON THE PRESS

Being harassed by the colectivos was a terrible experience; it happened in our offices of the federation of political scientists in the El Nacional building in downtown Caracas during Chávez's term, I presume that the objective of these thugs was to seize that building to then go through the headquarters of the printing press that was left in the farmhouses, but Chávez died, and Maduro arrived, who continued the plan, on that occasion he took the terror of the groups to the highest level.

I remember that on occasions, we had to hold our events at the El Nacional headquarters in Los Cortijos. The groups would show up around them burning tires, firing shots, showing their machetes and knives, and throwing bags of excrement at the entrance; this is what that Maduro ordered to do against the people of El Nacional, its journalists and workers, his obsession with staying with El Nacional led him to invent a slander in collaboration with the criminal Diosdado Cabello, together they seized the building and land through a court ruling Supreme Court of Justice of Maduro. In this way, El Nacional was taken from its rightful owners.

Concerning this crime by the Maduro regime, I wrote a post referring to what happened under the title "Letter to Luis Almagro: Let's invoke the role of the free press in the anniversary month of El Nacional," published on August 18, 2022, Here are some excerpts from my post:

"This time, I come to you on behalf of the Venezuelan Federation of Political Scientists on the occasion of highlighting the importance of the role played by the free press in favor of the fight for freedom and the maintenance of democracy on the continent. It is precise because of the free press that it has been possible for the world to be aware of the crimes committed by the Maduro regime.

The work of communication is fundamental in that sense. On the occasion of commemorating the month of the 79th anniversary of the newspaper El Nacional, I want to highlight its work as one of the prominent newspapers in the Hispanic world and a bulwark of Venezuelans.

As a political scientist, I envision El Nacional as a space where the defense of the truth and the emancipation of the people are possible. We Venezuelans know that, since its inception, its frontal position against dictatorships and tyrannies has earned the aversion of the regimes, first of Chávez and finally of Maduro.

The latter, Maduro, would take the newspaper to a rigged trial to close it. It is said that on February 7, 2021, when Judge Lisbeth del Carmen Amoroso Hidrobo awarded Diosdado Cabello ownership of the headquarters of El Nacional, Maduro proclaimed the closure of the free press in Venezuela.

The reality is that El Nacional is an institution that has survived the worst totalitarian regimes in our republican history, and Maduro will not be the exception

Mr. Almagro, I am going to allow myself to relate some personal experiences that I was able to witness regarding the actions of Maduro officials; it is about the siege of the facilities of both buildings owned by El Nacional, located in El Silencio and Los Cortijos, in For this reason, I would like to express that the experience was terrifying, I was able to see the attacks against the facilities, I was inside when they occurred, the attackers threw stones, bottles, bags with excrement against the doors, windows, and walls, I even heard fire detonations from weapons, there are no words to describe the atmosphere of horror that these Chavistas sowed, something that impressed me was seeing the mystique of the people of El Nacional; its journalists staying at their jobs, taking the information to the country, risking their lives.

Finally, in that letter, I say goodbye to Mr. Almagro, urging him to continue defending democracy on the continent and not to faint in accompanying those of us who fight for the freedom of our beloved

Venezuela.

A public letter was sent to Luis Almagro inviting him to invoke the role of the free press in the anniversary month of El Naciona

LIVING THE ASSAULT ON THE FEDERAL PALACE

Images of deputies and officials attacked during the assault on the Federal Parliament by groups at the service of Nicolas Maduro and Jorge Rodríguez.

With the arrival of 2017, everything began to collapse in Venezuela; Maduro's repression was reaching the highest levels, no matter how hard I tried to see the positive side; in fact, I remember that I was building a small inn just meters from a paradisiacal beach, in what for me meant a personal life project. However, the burden of the problems with the Maduro regime was such that they made it impossible to even think about having an everyday life.

The social conflict was increasing to levels never seen before. There were queues where we could spend up to 12 hours waiting to be seen to buy food and medicine. There were no plane tickets, we couldn't withdraw money from ATMs either, since a corralito system was imposed, there was no gasoline either, the regime had unleashed all its power to control the demonstrations and protests in the streets, which were repressed with rawness and savagery.

It was probably the worst year I know of in terms of repression against the opposition; a report from the Venezuelan Observatory of Social Conflict said that from April 1, 2017, to July 31, 2017, 6,729 demonstrations had been recorded throughout Venezuela, the equivalent of to 56 daily protests. We practically lived in a territory at war.

The conflict escalated to desperate levels; the streets were militarized, Maduro was totally paranoid, and it was precisely that year that I was invited to work in the National Assembly..

Left, AN 2015 employee credential, on the right side Esteban Oria during his conference before the congress of political scientists in the chamber of Deputies of the National Assembly, the year 2016

I joined the role of professional support in the technology department. I took this job, not for his salary; money was already being impacted by inflation, losing its face value at such a rate that it was worthless in real terms. The truth is that I took the job in solidarity with the opponents who defended the little democracy that remained in Venezuela, which at that time was represented in the National Assembly elected in 2015.

In my advisory role, I supported the office team on technological tools for social media management and digital marketing and some other considerations in which my support was requested.

WHEN FLEEING VENEZUELA BECOMES A QUESTION OF LIFE OR DEATH

At the end of June, the situation of the street conflict reached the labor offices within the National Assembly. They (followers of Maduro and Chavez) had turned the surroundings of the National Assembly and the Federal Palace into a war zone. The place had become increasingly dangerous. Going to the office in the administrative building meant avoiding military barbed wire, checkpoints, and checkpoints for supporters of the Maduro regime.

On the occasions that I went to the office or at home, I said goodbye with a see you later, you don't know. That was what it was about going to an office of the National Assembly, risking your life in front of any of these ill-tempered subjects that Maduro had stationed around the building to make life miserable for us, to the point of threatening and attacking every passerby who circulated to the Federal Palace.

It was precisely in the administrative building of the parliament known as José María Vargas in July 2017 that I had the opportunity to witness and be a victim of the most violent siege I have ever witnessed, and believe me, I had seen it all with the attacks we suffered in the Federation office in the former headquarters of El Nacional, but with the assault on the Federal Parliament, Maduro's followers reached a higher level of violence.

I was able to see and witness how a large group of fans of the Maduro regime entered the building, the headquarters of the parliamentary departments and the work commissions; They came to our administrative offices armed with baseball bats, tubes, and short weapons, they pounced on everyone present, we were pushed and savagely beaten. I remember seeing injured people lying on the ground, bleeding, and carnage.

Colonel Bladimir Humberto Lugo Armas was in charge of the National Guard; he was in charge of the custody of the José María Vargas building, the administrative headquarters of the parliament where we were; it was he who gave the order to open the doors and let people pass. the assailants and supporters of Maduro, who were under the leadership of Oswaldo Rivero, a popular TV presenter known as Cabeza e Mango.

Maduro decorated Colonel Lugo Armas for his support for the vandalism of the assault on the Federal Palace.

Unlike in 2016, when Jorge Rodríguez, current president of Maduro's National Assembly, was seen leading the siege of the National Assembly, in 2017, he commanded the assault from his office in the Caracas City Hall, right in front of the Federal Palace. He was the one who gave the orders to Cabeza e Mango and his followers to attack and attack us.

The assailants attacked women, the elderly, and children. I was among the officials who were able to escape through the basement of the administrative building; in my post entitled "Public letter to the European Parliament," published in El Nacional on August 12, 2022, I made a historical recount of the events that occurred during the siege and assault on Parliament, urging the chamber of the European Parliament not to legitimize the current National Assembly, whose current president Jorge Rodríguez had already sullied parliamentary institutions, for leading the assault on the Palace Fed twice.

In that post, I denounced that the Maduro regime has been skillful enough to buy the conscience of opposition deputies to betray the 2015 National Assembly, of which they were a voter to support and legitimize a new directive in Parliament to prepare the way for the arrival of recent parliamentary elections.

What Maduro did in 2019 was bribe deputies Luis Eduardo Parra Rivero, Jose Gregorio Noriega Figueroa, Franklyn Leonardo Duarte, Jose Dionisio Brito Rodriguez, Conrado Antonio Pérez Linares, Adolfo Ramón

Superlano and Negal Manuel Morales Llovera; these deputies along with those of the PSUV swore a false directive with Luis Parra as president.

Jorge Rodríguez leading the assault on the federal Parliament in 2016, currently the year 2022, is the president of the National Assembly in 2019

Then in 2020, with the approval of that directive of the National Assembly, Maduro called for parliamentary elections in December. His party, the PSUV, took control of the Parliament in Venezuela with more than 90% of the seats and an official abstention of 70%. They were the typical elections wrapped in accusations of fraud, without international support or participation of the opposition, fulfilling the objective of Chavismo to control the legislative power.

Then, the Maduro regime protected a group of its officials, including the military, who are subject to severe accusations for their alleged participation in crimes against humanity or drug trafficking, precisely sanctioned by the United States administration. The regime incorporated them into its lists of deputies, and they obtained their respective seats.

Mention some of them, it is General Suárez Chourio, who is sanctioned for several of these charges; General Quevedo also appears on the lists, as does Nicolás Maduro Guerra. Others mentioned are José Benavides Torres, who was the General Commander of the National Guard. He has international sanctions, pointed out for violation of Human

Rights. He is a representative for the Capital District. Admiral Giuseppe Alessandro Martin Alessandrello Cimadevilla was general commander of the Navy during the serious incident that occurred with the Resolute. He was previously head of REDI Central. He is the vice president of the discipline of the PSUV. Sanctioned by Canada, there are 15 other officials sanctioned by the United States and the European Union for corruption, money laundering, and human rights violations who won a seat in Parliament. This is what the Maduro regime is all about, controlling the powers through its administration by criminals and mafias; they rule Venezuela.

Regarding my post published in El Nacional entitled Letter to the European Parliament, I will share an excerpt with you: "So I can talk to you about the times of the assaults on Parliament, particularly the Chavista assault on Parliament in 2017. Before that, it is necessary that know the type of Parliament that supports Maduro. In principle, it comprises Chavista supporters sanctioned by the United States and the European Union. It is striking that Maduro has protected them with parliamentary immunity, knowing that they are a group of soldiers accused of being responsible for torture and repression against the dissent".

Then I continue in the post; "In this sense, I share with you what an investigation by the newspaper Infobae says and that I am going to allow myself to copy an extract of its content: This is the case of Major General Antonio Benavides Torres, accused by the prosecutor Luisa Ortega Díaz 'for the alleged commission of serious and systematic violations of human rights' against the anti-government demonstrations that left more than 150 dead and thousands injured and detained in 2018, Ortega Díaz denounced him before the International Criminal Court for having committed 'crimes of murder, torture, imprisonment, as well as a systematic and generalized attack against the population.' According to the Infobae portal, other designated deputies are General Jesús Suárez Chourio, who was sanctioned by the United States for his responsibility in the violence and repression against anti-government protests and sanctioned by the European Union for the repression against opponents, major Francisco

Ameliach, who was accused of being responsible for the murder of the student Génesis Carmona. Major General Manuel Quevedo, former president of PDVSA and former Minister of Petroleum. In 2019 he was sanctioned by the United States and accused of being responsible for corrupt schemes at PDVSA. General Giuseppe Alesandrello Cimadevilla, In 2019 was sanctioned by Canada for his responsibility in the repression and persecution of interim government members, censorship, and excessive use of force against civil society. Lieutenant Diosdado Cabello led the illegitimate constituent assembly that dedicated itself to undermining the National Assembly, persecuting its deputies, violating their parliamentary immunity, and ordering their imprisonment. In March 2020, he was indicted by the United States Department of Justice on charges of narcoterrorism, drug trafficking, and weapons. Pedro Carreño was sanctioned by the United States for his links with the repression against opponents and the Chavista regime's corruption. José Gregorio Vielma Mora, sanctioned by the United States for the evil plot of the CLAP food boxes".

"So Maduro managed to strip the legitimate parliamentarians of their seats and parliament building to install his group of deputies, sanctioned by the international community for crimes against human rights, but it must also be added that he places himself as president of the Assembly National to the architect of the sieges and assaults on Parliament, Jorge Rodríguez." End of extract.

The situation we experienced in the National Assembly during 2017 was tremendously stressful; you probably have no idea, dear readers, what it means to be an opposition official with your office in the heart of Caracas, inside the administrative building of the National Assembly, in that period. As I have narrated in previous lines, all of us who worked in those offices lived with great anguish. Precisely when Maduro besieged parliament, the truth is that it was in an environment of extreme violence.

There were these guys, the colectivos, many of them were officials of the National Assembly that we saw and ran into daily in the offices; some were union members, they were the ones promoting this violence, the guard protected them, and they did everything possible to sabotage the parliamentary administration.

Every day we were exposed to these threats, so amid this trauma, I decided to take some time to return to what I knew in the past as an environment of relative neutrality and tolerance; it was my lodge; I was supposed to In Freemasonry, we avoid the debate of politics and religion, precisely because we try to make space for healthy coexistence, perhaps my idea was to go back to have a coffee with old friends.

It was common to see Freemasons on both sides of the political spectrum, with the behavior of tolerance, despite our differences; however, what was to happen to us would be the most vivid expression of the reach of the Maduro regime and its effects. All that class hatred had reached our temples to the point that I wanted to have a good time with old friends, which led to something much worse than what we experienced in the National Assembly or our Fedepolitologos offices.

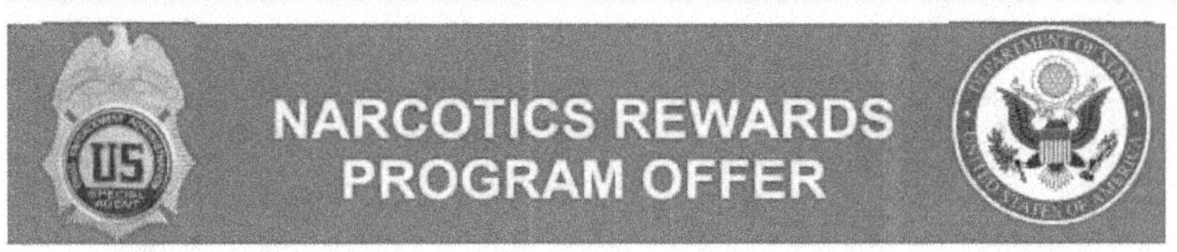

The Department of State Bureau of International Narcotics and Law Enforcement Services (INL) Offers

Reward of up to $10,000,000 United States dollars

for Information Leading to Arrest/Conviction

Of

Diosdado Cabello Rondon

Contact the DEA with any tips by phone or e-mail:

Phone/Text/WhatsApp/Telegram/Signal: +1-202-681-8187

Email: CartelSolesTips@usdoj.gov

Diosdado Cabello poster published on the DEA

RETURNING TO THE LODGE

Oscar Pérez posing at the entrance of the Grand Lodge of Venezuela

The siege of our Venezuelan Federation of Political Scientists offices at the headquarters of El Nacional and the assault on the National Assembly were terrifying experiences. In 2017, the assault that Maduro's hordes made on our offices in the executive building of Parliament was fresh in my memory, which left me very disturbed.

Maduro's mobs unleashed all their violence, resulting in hundreds of injuries; All these vandal actions were carried out under the command of Jorge Rodríguez, with the collaboration of the commander of the military garrison that guarded the federal palace, Colonel Bladimir Lugo.

I was quite worried and shocked. There was a lot of political violence around me, and I knew I was in a risky position; there was this other thorny issue of espionage and state surveillance; in short, 2017 was a year that accumulated bad experiences.

Despite not having been arrested by the security forces, unlike other of my opposition colleagues, the truth is that I always felt that for me, it was a matter of time before they arrested me under any pretext.

At the end of the first quarter of 2017, looking for some peace, I approached my lodge Santiago Mariño Number 208; after more than ten years of retirement, I asked for my reinstatement, which was granted.

The idea of visiting my lodge was to meet old friends, including some Chavistas. Indeed, we were politically adverse, but we never brought partisan politics to our workshops; we always respected political differences and treated each other as brothers; that is what Freemasonry is all about, asserting virtues such as tolerance; however, that year, 2017 politics Maduro and his war had come to our order.

As is natural, after so long without going to a place, when we return, we always meet old friends and new ones. The lodge Santiago Mariño Number 208 was characterized by being small in the number of members. On the occasion of my arrival, I noticed the presence of a group of new apprentices; of all of them, I want to highlight two names, Oscar Pérez and José Diaz Pimentel, who was going to imagine that this small lodge, almost unknown in the Masonic world, it was going to become a powder keg in a matter of days.

The lodge meetings were held on Saturday mornings in a temple workshop located in Jesuitas a Maturín. Before opening the works, each member commissioned him by the duties of a Freemason. These two young men, Oscar and Pimentel, stood out in the group of apprentices, particularly for their commitment to learning and collaborating.

Despite being apprentices, they were allowed to participate with readings or plates; these guys were a revelation; Oscar Pérez caught my attention due to the strength of his speeches, which were accompanied by a bearing of martiality and poise. The young man promised a lot for the new generations.

I learned about his philanthropic work; he visited and helped sick children in hospitals, giving them medicines and gifts at Christmas; he was a great philanthropist. He is also an artist and a television personality. In 2015 he acted in a film titled "Death Suspended"; he was the public image of the CICPC police for institutional programs. Surprisingly, we had this character in our modest lodge, and he was a celebrity.

The photo was taken in the white outfit on June 24, 2017, from left to right Igor Oswaldo Alcalá Merino, Oscar Pérez, Johnny Calderon, and Jameson Jiménez.

Oscar always showed courtesy and humility; he was there providing his services in his apprenticeship without asking for any kind of special treatment, simply doing his job and receiving instructions from his respective guard; sometimes, he was seen stoically sitting in a martial attitude to waiting for his turn or keeping his work following the instruction norm, in short, from me he undoubtedly obtained an outstanding grade.

I could share conversations with Oscar Pérez on several occasions while we sat in the bush or when we were in the antechamber of the workshop. We agreed on the need for political change and the rescue of the democratic system; we agreed that the Maduro regime was a dictatorship. In these conversations, I got the impression that I was in front of a Freemason who had the style of the Freemasons in the times of Bolívar and Miranda, extreme cordiality while maintaining an icy gaze; his frankness did not break his kindness. When he gave his readings in the lodge, we could see that we were facing a jewel of incalculable value for modern Freemasonry; his tone of voice and Templar gaze amazed those present; little did it realize that this young man would become a revelation as a new emerging leader of the Venezuelan opposition for national and international politics.

A BIT OF MY PAST IN FREEMASONRY

I have been a Freemason for at least 20 years or more; I started in the lodge Santiago Mariño Number 208, affiliated with the Grand Lodge of Venezuela, located on the corner of Jesuitas to Maturín in Caracas.

Simón Bolivar Palacios, se sabe que recibió al grado de Compañero en la muy respetable madre logia de San Alejandro de Escocia. En el museo masónico de New York se encuentra el mandil y el collarín de Bolívar correspondientes a su Grado 32.

Simón Bolívar Palacios is known that he received the Degree of Companion in the very respectable mother lodge of San Alejandro de Escocia. In the Masonic museum of New York are the apron and collar of Bolívar corresponding to his 32nd Degree.

I became a Freemason because the heroes of independence always caught my attention; most of them were Freemasons. In Venezuela, 39 of the great men who rest in the national pantheon were Freemasons, to mention a few Francisco de Miranda Rodríguez (cenotaph), Antonio José de Sucre Alcalá (cenotaph), Andrés Bello López (cenotaph), Andrés Eloy

Blanco Iturbe, Antonio Guzmán Blanco, Santiago Mariño Carige, Luis Razetti Martínez, José Félix Ribas Herrera, Carlos Soublette Jerez, Diego Bautista Urbaneja Sturdy, Simón Rodríguez and Simón Bolívar Palacios.

George Washington On September 18, 1793, he laid the cornerstone of the United States Capitol wearing the Masonic regalia of a Grand Master.

In the United States, at least 18 of the 56 signers of the Declaration of Independence were known Freemasons: John Hancock, who was president of Congress; Samuel Adams; John Adams; William Ellery; Benjamin Franklin; Elbridge Gerry; Lyman Hall; Joseph Hewes; William Hopper; Thomas Jefferson; Thomas Nelson Jr.; Robert Treat Paine; John Penn; George Read; Roger Sherman; Richard Stockton; George Walton and William Whipple. We must add 15 presidents, among which is its first president George Washington.

Great politicians, scientists, soldiers, and musicians like Mozart were part of the ranks of Freemasonry; in short, I felt a great attraction for these characters, and thus my interest in starting in this organization was born, which had been not only an inspiration, but also a home. of these great personalities.

Esteban Oria in the center, left the master Alirio Oramas in the cap of the Grand Lodge of Venezuela.

It was precisely an art giant who invited me, it was the master Alirio Oramas, a personality in Venezuelan art, winner of the national painting prize in 1951, he was part of the group of artists who would later meet in Paris under the name of Los Disidentes, among which the names of Alejandro Otero, Mateo Manaure, Narciso Debourg, Pascual Navarro stood out.

Alirio Oramas participated in the arts integration project of the Ciudad Universitaria de Caracas, directed by the architect Carlos Raúl Villanueva, with five murals whose central theme is the progression of color. It was an honor to have been sponsored by this figure of art. Venezuelan.

During my first years as a Freemason I was collaborating in the Grand Lodge. I could probably say that one of the best moments lived was during the period in which the Grand Mastery was directed by General Víctor Higuera Castellano, a wise man, very talented. I understand that during his administration the initiation of Hugo Chávez was prevented. So we made a lot of audiovisual material to support the order and I was quite involved with its dissemination.

Masonic passport of Esteban Oria

Another pleasant memory was visiting the Esperanza N° 7 del Este lodge, where our good friend, the late brother Ramón Diaz, received us. Frankly, we had a great time with these brothers and friends sharing topics of interest, lots of talk, culture and knowledge.

Then other great teachers arrived and I observed that the distances with the populist government of Chávez were shortening more and more, so it seemed better to me to go in a dream, they were more than 10 years separated from my lodge, which I dedicated to my university studies, politics and business, and it was not until 2017 that I returned for the aforementioned reasons; I decided to return to the Santiago Mariño N 208 lodge, which was my right, since it is the place where I began in Freemasonry.

JOSE ESTEBAN ORIA

THE RISING OF AN OPPOSITIONER WHO IS A MASON

Oscar Pérez called for rebellion against Maduro's tyranny in June 2016; in his speech, his first words were Dear Brothers.

Oscar Pérez called for rebellion against Maduro's tyranny in June 2016; in his speech, his first words were Dear Brothers.

Everything was normally going in the lodge until, on June 27, 2017, we saw a video that showed Oscar Pérez and armed men asking for Maduro's resignation; he said at that time, "we are nationalists, patriots, and institutionalists. This fight is not with the rest of the state forces; it is against the tyranny of this government. Of course, receiving Oscar's video in the lodge's WhatsApp group chat was a surprise. He regularly used it to find out about the brothers' messages, but this time it was a disruption; in the chat feed was the video of Oscar announcing to the world that he was rebelling against the tyrant Maduro.

I remember the last time I saw him was Saturday, June 24, 2017, three days before his act of rebellion, in a white outfit in the Grand Lodge; I did not stay for that act, I left early, even before it started, but I managed to see Oscar Pérez on the stairs at the doors of the Great Temple, precisely him entering and me leaving, we shook hands; I told him I was leaving, that I'm not good at protocol acts, he seemed to understand me with his smile, anyway, it was the last time.

The video had been sent from his telephone number; I was paralyzed and shocked, in principle, because I knew of the implications that it could bring us with the Maduro police, in the sense that in that Chat, there were intelligence officials, of course, they were Freemason brothers, but this situation could get out of hand and turn it over to the security officials of the Maduro regime. For these reasons for using Chat, the Maduro regime creates suspects and arrests innocent people by inventing their stories and opening a file. Even though we had nothing to do with Oscar's action, we could receive retaliation for that reason; this was what first worried me.

Regarding Oscar's act, I want to state that my first impression was the same as that of most Venezuelans; I celebrated that someone had finally taken the audacity to confront the tyrant of Miraflores. Naturally quite worried because Oscar was a member of our lodge, and he had no idea what the consequences would be, but I sensed that he had to prepare for the worst.

Everything was happening very quickly; I remembered the times I read on my sheets in the lodge urging the Masons to have a more critical attitude towards what was happening in Venezuela; Oscar Pérez went further, with his oath as a Freemason, the same thing we do when closing our work in the lodge, which quotes "Eternal repudiation of tyrants and tyrannies," he interpreted it in concrete actions.

The vast majority of Venezuelans applauded the action of Oscar Pérez; they were convinced that Maduro deserved to be removed from power; he was a ruler who had murdered more than 200 protesters between 2014 and 2017 during mass protests, he had given instructions to his guard and militia groups to open fire on innocent people, he was a confessed criminal.

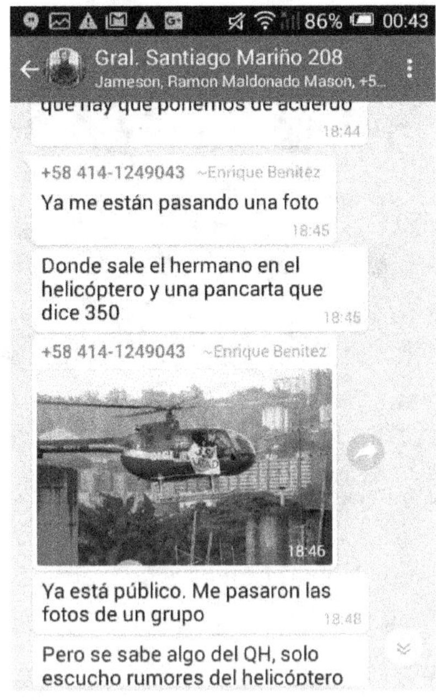

Screenshots of the WhatsApp group of the moment Oscar Pérez sends his message where he rebels against Maduro.

Maduro gave weapons to his paramilitaries called colectivos to attack, shoot and kill people in the protests; he also killed the popular leaders of the neighborhoods to silence the demonstrations. Oscar Pérez did an act of justice appealing to article 350 of the Bolivarian Constitution of Venezuela.

What Article 350 says: In Chapter III – Of the National Constituent Assembly, it states: "The people of Venezuela, faithful to its republican tradition, to its struggle for independence, peace, and freedom, will disregard any regime, legislation or authority that goes against democratic values, principles, and guarantees or undermines human rights."

Oscar Pérez, who was a member of the CICPC's Special Actions Brigade, had interpreted that article 350 of the constitution empowered him to ignore the regime of Nicolás Maduro for the reasons mentioned above.

On Jan 17, 2018, a special on Maduro came out in the German press (Spiegel) under the title "El Carnicero."

Oscar's video quickly went viral and positioned him as a new actor in the opposition. By appealing to constitutional 350, he acted politically, the opposite of the regime's narrative that labeled him a terrorist.

The truth is that it is not known that Oscar Pérez used his weapons to cause casualties in the state security forces; there was not a single injury that was attributed to him as a consequence of his actions; on the contrary, we saw that he used microphones and cameras to create awareness in the population, I understand that it was generating a critical mass that was growing and would soon be a majority capable of displacing and ousting Maduro from power.

Oscar Pérez was very critical even of some members of the Venezuelan opposition, whom he accused of complicity or being part of the corruption; on this argument, the facts over time have shown that he was right, in the sense that the opposition expressed in the political parties is largely responsible for keeping Maduro in power, many of them have betrayed the popular will by accepting bribes from Maduro and selling out to totalitarianism, it was the case of the election of members of the parliamentary board that displacement of legitimately elected officials in 2015, which was carried out fraudulently with the help of 18 "opposition" deputies who supported the strategy of the dictatorship of Nicolás Maduro in the National Assembly. Then there is the overthrow of the interim government of Guaido by an alliance of the three major parties, UNT, AD, and PJ, in an action that is being scrutinized because, in the opinion of jurists, it is an illegal act that puts The maintenance of international sanctions against Maduro, given that account, forces countries to institutionally recognize a dictatorship like Maduro's, since there is no legal counterweight in the opposition.

So years before, in 2017, Oscar Pérez raised his voice for his people to ask Maduro to resign; I think he was facing practically alone, with the support of a small group, all of them fighting against an armed and murderous regime like the of Maduro.

El caso de Óscar Pérez desata el espionaje militar contra los masones en Venezuela

POR ANTONIO JOSÉ CHINCHETRU — 1 DE NOVIEMBRE DE 2017 EN ACTUALIDAD, VENEZUELA

Antonio José Chinchetru (ALN).- El servicio de contraespionaje militar venezolano ha puesto en el punto de mira a la masonería del país, de la que era miembro el expolicía Óscar Pérez, líder de los rebeldes muertos en la masacre de El Junquito. Según denuncia la Gran Logia de España citando a sus correligionarios venezolanos, los espías del Ejército chavista han comenzado a elaborar un censo de los masones del país y a investigar sus actividades.

Óscar Pérez, el expolicía jefe del grupo rebelde cuyos miembros murieron la semana pasada en la masacre de El Junquito (al oeste de Caracas), había sido miembro de la masonería hasta su expulsión este 9 de enero, días antes de que fuera abatido. Coincidiendo con la operación en la que la Policía Nacional Bolivariana (PNB) y paramilitares de los 'colectivos' chavistas acabaron con su vida, el espionaje militar de Venezuela ha comenzado una operación para establecer un censo de masones en el país.

La masonería española teme que sea "el preludio de la depuración sistemática de nuestros Queridos Hermanos"

La Dirección General de Contrainteligencia Militar de Venezuela ha puesto en marcha una operación "para conocer la membresía, direcciones físicas de los templos y formación impartida en diversas Logias de la Masonería Venezolana", según ha contado la Gran Logia de España – Grande Oriente Español en un correo electrónico en el que cita como fuente a las logias del país suramericano. La comunicación de la Gran Logia de España añade: "Las Logias que nos han contactado han sido informadas por los agentes

Press headline: The case of Óscar Pérez unleashes military espionage against Freemasons in Venezuela

OSCAR'S REBELLION PUT PRESSURE ON FREEMASONRY

Naturally, I was concerned by the fact that regime officials were added to the Chat where we received Oscar's video; some were even militiamen, but until then, we had had cordial relations in the lodge, and Freemasonry had not taken an official position in favor of the Maduro regime, even during the protests, at least it is my appreciation.

The Chavista Freemasons had shown themselves to be tolerant; I would never have thought that a scenario would be generated within the lodge in which the interests of the Maduro regime would affect us to the extreme of putting our lives at risk; however, times change, and it was precisely what happened after Oscar Pérez released his video.

So after Oscar's rebellion, from the moment we received his video in the Chat, not three hours passed when I was answering a call from the venerable Master of the Lodge, brother Rubén Rodríguez, with a somewhat broken and worrying tone of voice. , to let me know that due to pressure from the Grand Fiscal Speaker, a high official of the Grand Lodge, he had allegedly been instructed to open a Masonic trial against Oscar Pérez to expel him from the lodge.

I knew the seriousness of the matter immediately; during the conversation, I just listened to him. Finally, Rubén invited me to Oscar's irradiation meeting (meeting or assembly), which will occur on the Saturday following our conversation.

That conversation with Rubén confirmed my concern about the possible consequences of Oscar's rebellion within Freemasonry, but it also brought me back to that state of stress from which he was trying to escape. In the lodge and Grand Lodge, the mourners began to show up in the regime, and they began to act accordingly. They were already on alert due to my recent experiences in the National Assembly, but now the situation was becoming much more alarming and worrying since we were beginning to be directly affected by a new political situation that seemed highly explosive.In the lodge and Grand Lodge, the mourners began to show up in the regime, and they began to act accordingly.

Capture de pantalla del grupo de WhatsApp. mensaje enviado dese phone de Oscar Pérez

Mensaje de los hermanos mostrando incredulidad en el acto de Oscar

FEAR TURNED THEM INTO COLLABORATORS

I watched as control gave way to fear; from one moment to the next, Oscar Pérez was declared a practically public enemy. Oscar made a personal decision; at no time did he mention the Freemasons or Freemasonry; however, according to Rubén, obeying the guidelines of the Grand Fiscal Speaker of the Grand Lodge, they ordered him to make that trial to expel Oscar, pretending that with this act of alleged collaboration with the regime, we would be forgiven for entering its military intelligence radar.

Rubén Rodríguez, past venerable Master of the lodge Santiago Mariño N 208

Without us knowing it, in July, there was already a Freemason named Ramon Delgado, an apprentice member of our Santiago Mariño lodge, who the DGCIM had arrested in the first days of July. In his statement before the military judge, He mentioned Freemasonry on three occasions, probably a statement under duress, and he had involved us.

And concerning the tea of the Masonic trials, I want to draw attention to its use by totalitarian regimes; the Grand Master of Cuba denounced this type of method, Francisco Javier Alfonso Vidal, who escaped from the security of Cubans for an event in Mexico the first days of January 2023, what Vidal said was that the Canel regime gave him the order to make a Masonic trial of the Grand Commander Viñas Alonso, to expel him, probably with the intention that the Cuban state security agencies. But what the Grand Master of Cuba did was escape from the Cubans in Mexico, and then in the United States, he denounced all these hoaxes and requested asylum.

When I found out about the trial against Oscar, I understood that the Maduro regime was operating within the Grand Lodge in principle through this man mentioned by Rubén, the Grand Fiscal Speaker, later I would know that this matter of collaboration came from a higher level, by Grand

Master Ubaldo Jiménez Silva, already in those days of July I practically went underground. Naturally, I did not attend the trial.

At the time of Oscar's rebellion, the lodge's group chat was closed by Jameson Jiménez; later, I learned that he opened another discussion, where I was added. In this way, I could follow what was happening in the lodge from my exile.

A CONTROVERSIAL DOCUMENT

A statement presumably signed by the Past Grand Master Colonel Juan Ubaldo Jiménez and by the Past Grand Secretary Alfredo Tovar gives an account of the orientation taken by the Grand Lodge during the act of rebellion by Oscar Pérez; in the said document, they argue that according to the Article 15 of the constitution of the Grand Lodge, they are empowered to impeach Oscar Pérez and declare that he has lost his status as a Freemason, for the reason that the Maduro regime has declared him a traitor to the country.

The truth is that no Freemason loses his status as a lodge member in any circumstance in which he appeals to his freedom of conscience.

Under no circumstances can a member be thrown out of the workshop, undermine their rights, and even less become part of a conspiracy or plot to compromise their reputation or support a lawsuit to favor the relationship with an outlaw state like Maduro's to the detriment of the rights of a brother of the workshop.

I want to reiterate that the Maduro regime has been repeatedly accused of systematically violating the human rights of thousands of Venezuelan citizens; it has been denounced before the UN Human Rights Council, which has created a Mission that investigates it exclusively to follow up On his transgressions, precisely the latest report denounces him for crimes against humanity, the most severe crime that a state can commit.

Authorities of the Grand Lodge 2014 - 2017, from left to right, Grand Master Colonel National Guard Juan Ubaldo Jiménez Silva, Grand Secretary Alfredo Tovar

Press reports say that in some of these documented cases, "the detained women and men were subjected to one or more forms of torture" with "the application of electric current, suffocation with plastic bags, simulated drowning, beatings, sexual violence, deprivation of water and food, forced postures and exposure to extreme temperatures," details the document, pointing out that the Bolivarian Intelligence Service (SEBIN) and the General Directorate of Military Counterintelligence (DGCIM) are responsible for these practices.

Then there is the report of the independent UN Mission of 2020 that urges the Venezuelan state to render accounts for crimes against humanity. (https://www.ohchr.org/es/2020/09/venezuela-un-report-urges-accountability-crimes-against-humanity)

The Mission says it investigated 223 cases, of which 48 are included as comprehensive case studies in the 443-page report. Additionally, the Mission examined another 2,891 cases to corroborate the patterns of violations and crimes. It identified highly coordinated patterns of violations and crimes by State policies and part of a generalized and systematic course of conduct, thus constituting crimes against humanity. It verified that the Government, State agents, and the groups that worked with them had committed flagrant violations of the human rights of men and women in Venezuela.

Finally, another of the documents that I want to refer to is the report of the Mission for the year 2022 (https://www.ohchr.org/es/press-releases/2022/09/venezuela-new-un-report-details-responsibilities -crimes-against-humanity).

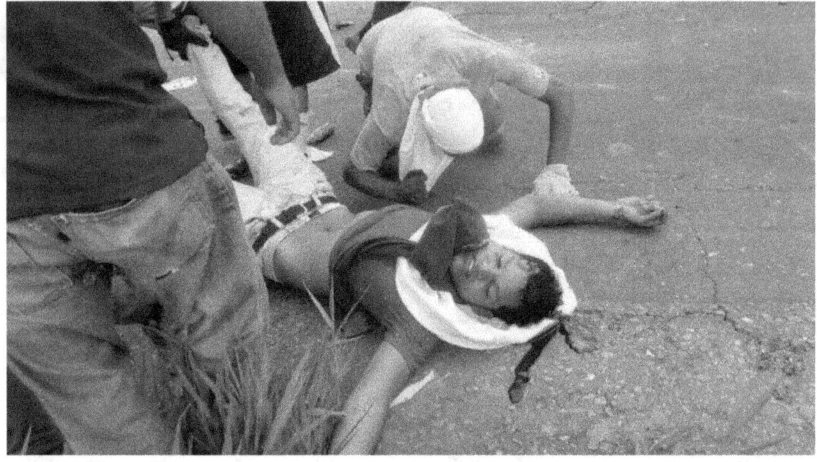

Another shot to the head during the repression of the Maduro military regime against civil demonstrations

The report says that the intelligence agencies of the State of Venezuela, both civilian and military, function as well-coordinated and effective structures for the execution of a plan, orchestrated from the highest levels of the government, to repress dissent through the commission of crimes against humanity.

"Our investigations and analysis show that the Venezuelan state uses intelligence services and their agents to suppress dissent. This leads to the commission of serious crimes and human rights violations, including acts of torture and sexual violence. These practices must cease immediately, and those responsible must be investigated and prosecuted in accordance with the law," said Marta Valiñas, president of the UN fact-finding mission.

So the Venezuelan state under the usurped presidency of Maduro was sunk in the mire of the systematic violation of human rights; in 2017, the same repressive state that Maduro ruled had murdered more than 200 protesters in the streets, using death squads like the collectives, who were armed with weapons of war and launched against unarmed citizens.

Through television, we witnessed the transmission of images showing crude demonstrators during the protests with open wounds when they were taken to hospitals that had collapsed due to many injuries.

It was known that after protests at night, Maduro agents raided the houses and homes that they identified as the leaders' homes to kidnap them and take them before military courts without due process to be prosecuted for crimes of treason. To the homeland, with false accusations of attempting to overthrow Maduro.

Venezuelans have always been aware of the Venezuelan state's continued use of these bad legal practices. Therefore, it should never have lent itself to a Masonic trial of this political nature against Oscar Pérez, a lodge attached to the Grand Lodge of Venezuela during those administrations of 2017-2018.

THE ALLEGED COLLABORATION OF THE PAST GRAN MAESTRO AND THE ACTIONS OF THE REGIME OF MADURO

Regarding the trial, a witness told me that a quorum could not be achieved, so what they did was a round table. They asked those present whether or not they wanted to disaffiliate Oscar, and the majority of the workshop voted for not disaffiliating Oscar. Oscar.

The venerable maestro Rubén Rodríguez did not abide by the verdict on one occasion; I understand that at the end of July, Oscar was present at the workshop; on that date, I was in a low profile and was not going to the lodge, witnesses tell me that the venerable maestro Rubén Rodríguez together with two other dignities of the workshop, the tax speaker and the expert brother, one of them I will mention his initials AE, the other brother is deceased, it was brother Ricardo Torres, finally the three made the decision to deny him the access to Oscar Pérez, the Pérez and Pimentel brothers were left outside the workshop, in the street in danger exposed to Maduro's hunters.

I want to explain from the Masonic point of view why a Masonic trial should never have been raised against Oscar; this matter is typified in the constitutions of the Freemasons of 1723 that cite the following:

Of the duties of a Freemason. From Chapter II Of the Head of State and his subordinates.

"… So, if a brother rebels against the State, he must not support him in his rebellion, even if he is sorry for such a misfortune; and if he is not convicted of any crime, even if the loyal Fraternity should condemn the rebellion and not give the Government the slightest reason for suspicion or the slightest foundation in the matter, they will not be able to expel him from the Lodge, and his relationship with it remains unbroken.".

This law is more than two hundred years old; by the time it was drafted, it constituted a significant advance; it was about the recognition of the right of conscience and rebellion in a period governed by absolute monarchies, even at that time, the order understood the fact that a rebellious act of one of its members could result in serious harm to all, that their recommendation was not to become part of the conflict, but under no circumstances should a brother be sacrificed, for this reason, they do not accept for any reason that the rebellious member is unaffiliated or separated from the workshop.

Since the writing of Anderson's constitutions, there have been significant changes in constitutional law, so to have an adequate interpretation of these boundaries, it is necessary to reconcile them with the legality of the updated environment, both in the field of national laws of the countries and concerning international treaties and conventions on human rights so that in case of deciding, common sense and the laws that endure prevailing and not immediacy.

It is customary for Freemasons to respect and take advantage of the laws of the countries where their lodges operate. Naturally, we are referring to democratic nations, where there is a division of powers, and their authorities are legitimately elected by popular will. Otherwise, it is impossible to benefit from a system of laws from a dictatorial regime, as occurs in Venezuela, where there are no independent public powers; everything depends on Maduro and his entourage or environment.

In Venezuela, judicial institutions are subordinated to an executive denounced as a criminal, nullifying the constitutional guarantees they offer citizens. Therefore, the value of national laws is pyrrhic.

Laws such as the Organic Law of Partial Reform of the Organic Code of Military Justice or the Venezuelan Penal Code are two legal instruments used in Maduro's judicial system to issue thousands of sentences against Venezuelan dissidents and political prisoners. Therefore, they are worthless Pyrrhic instances.

Regarding the crime of treason, so used in most of the sentences of the Maduro courts, the wording of the legal instrument says that "in the

Venezuelan Penal Code it is established as treason to conspire against the integrity of the territory of the country." country or against its republican institutions, or harass it by any means for any of these purposes; assist inside or outside Venezuela, with or without complicity, against the independence or integrity of the geographical space of the Republic. Likewise, it determines that whoever favors, facilitates, or helps directly or indirectly through acts of disturbance of public order, the plans of foreign enemies will also be infringing on the crime of treason against the homeland.

Alfredo Tovar, Grand Secretary of the Grand Lodge, is the alleged author of a condemnatory letter for crimes of treason against Oscar Pérez.

Article 132 of said Law adds that it is a crime of treason against the homeland the acts of those people who, inside or outside the national territory, conspire to destroy the republican political form or in which "request foreign intervention in the affairs of the domestic policy of Venezuela, or asks for its help to upset the peace of the Republic or that in front of its officials, or through publications made in the foreign press, incites civil war in the Republic or defames its President or insults the diplomatic representative or consular officials of Venezuela, because of their functions, in the country where the act was committed."

So it is through these legal instruments that the courts have executed these thousands of sentences arbitrarily against opponents. The Maduro regime accused Oscar Pérez and his collaborators of being traitors to the country. The accusatory argument used by the Maduro regime against Oscar Pérez and José Pimentel was replicated in an alleged document circulated in the lodge, signed by the Grand Master, Colonel of the National Guard Ubaldo Jiménez Silva, circulated between June and July 2017. I transcribed part of it below:

The Very Resp:. Grand Master of the Very respectable Grand Lodge of the Republic of Venezuela R:.H:. JUAN UBALDO JIMENEZ SILVA, under the Powers with which he is invested and by the Authority of Law on behalf of the Masonic High Chamber of Justice, I fulfill the duty to issue this statement,

CONSIDERING

1. The constitution of the Grand Lodge of the Republic of Venezuela in its articles 4, title IV, of the rite of freemasons expresses, "All men regularly initiated in one of the Lodges of the Jurisdiction of the Republic of Venezuela are freemasons, or in any other workshop in the jurisdiction of a regular Masonic Power" and article 16 "Every Freemason, even if he is not affiliated, is subject to the government of the fraternity and can be tried and punished by any of the Lodges of the jurisdiction where he resides.".

2. Article 18 of the title mentioned above specifies, "The duties of Freemasons are: 1) To ensure the Integrity of the Homeland, 2) Obey the laws of the country where they live, and 3) Respect the honor and property of others. In the same way, Article 20 mentions, "The quality of Freemason is lost: 1) for treason against the country, 2) For a dishonorable action; and that whose loss of said quality takes place in a final sentence pronounced in a Masonic Trial by article 21 of our constitution.

3. That one of the attributions as Grand Master under the provisions of the Positive Legal Order is to act as Judge and preside over the court to the Statute of Masonic Trial.

AGREEMENT AND TERM

Hold trial against Q:.H:. Oscar Alberto Pérez, Identity Card N 15943499, after evaluating the conduct in the different events where dear brother Oscar Alberto… End of the appointment.

In this letter, Ubaldo Jiménez Silva and Alfredo Tovar are allegedly signing. Both deny having signed this letter and argue that it is fake or false. By the way, it should be noted that brother Tovar is mentioned in another event that involves him in an alleged concealment of information about an investigation that he requested to do, and which resulted in the alleged forced disappearance of two other Masons, the outcome of this event it culminated in the persecution and exile of its researcher, later I will make a complete mention of this fact.

Francmasoneria Regular Universal R∴E∴A∴A∴   Familia Venezolana

A∴L∴ A∴ G∴ D∴ G∴ A∴ D∴ U∴

Gran Logia de la República de Venezuela

Instalada el 24 de Junio de 1824 (E∴ V∴) | Constitución de 1824 – Personería Jurídica desde 1944
Miembro de la Confederación de Grandes Logias Regulares del Mundo - Miembro de Confederación
Masónica Interamericana (C.I.M.) Miembro de Confederación Masónica Bolivariana (C.M.B.)
Gran Templo Masónico, Jesuitas a Maturín Nº 5 Caracas Venezuela Monumento Histórico Nacional
Teléfonos (0212) 8608548 -8605776 Fax (02) 8605776
Apartado de correos 827 - Caracas 1010-A Venezuela
Internet: http://www.granlogia.org.ve

COMUNICADO Nº92

El Muy Resp∴ Gran Maestro de la Muy Respetable Gran Logia de la República de Venezuela R∴H∴JUAN UBALDO JIMENEZ SILVA, en virtud de los Poderes con que esta investido y por Autoridad de la Ley en representación de la Alta Cámara de Justicia Masónica, cumplo con el deber de emitir el presente comunicado.

CONSIDERANDO

1. La Constitución de la GRAN LOGIA DE LA REPUBLICA DE VENEZUELA, en sus Artículos 6, Título IV del Rito de los Francmasones que expresa "Son francmasones todos los hombres regularmente iniciados en una de las Logias de la Jurisdicción de la Gran Logia de la República de Venezuela, o en cualquier otro taller de la jurisdicción de una Potencia Masónica Regular" y el Articulo 16 "Todo masón, aunque no estuviere afiliado, está sujeto al gobierno de la fraternidad y puede ser juzgado y penado por cualquiera de las Logias den la Jurisdicción donde resida"

2. Que el Articulo 18 del mencionado antes mencionado título especifica "Los deberes de los Francmasones son: 1) Velar por la integridad de la Patria, 2) Obedecer las leyes del pais donde viven, y 3) Respetar el honor y la propiedad ajena. Del mismo modo el Articulo 20 que menciona "La cualidad de Mason se pierde: 1) por traición a la Patria, 2) Por una acción deshonrosa; y que cuya perdida de dicha cualidad tiene lugar en sentencia firme pronunciada en Juicio Masónico de acuerdo al articulo 21 del nuestra constitución.

3. Que una de las atribuciones como Gran Maestro de acuerdo con lo establecido en el Ordenamiento Juridico Positivo es actuar como Juez y presidir el tribunal conforme al Estatuto de Enjuiciamiento Masónico.

ACUERDO Y DETERMINO

1. Celebrar enjuiciamiento en contra del Q∴H∴ Oscar Alberto Pérez Cedula de Identidad Nº 15948499, luego de la evaluar la conducta en los diferentes acontecimientos donde el Q∴H∴ Oscar Alberto

MASONERÍA EN ACCIÓN Y EVOLUCIÓN

The document that condemns Oscar Pérez as a traitor to the country was allegedly issued by Colonel Juan Ubaldo Jiménez, Past Grand Master of the Grand Lodge of Venezuela

PROSECUTOR ADMITS TRIAL AGAINST OSCAR

Regarding the trial against Oscar, a communication that was sent to me at the time by the prosecutor speaker of the AE lodge tried to justify Oscar's alleged non-affiliation based on the legal system in force in Venezuela, committing the terrible mistake of not understanding that the scope of the national legal system under Maduro's rules is in apparent contradiction with international humanitarian law and that no lodge should be attached to or obey that legal system but international conventions on human rights.

The brother prosecutor speaker argues, and I quote: "Anywhere on the planet a person who steals a helicopter and starts firing automatic weapons of war and dropping bombs on an open city, is accused of being a TERRORIST (...) 3) Brother Oscar he was never irradiated from the Order by the Lodge. I remind you that Article 16 of the Constitution of Venezuela reads as follows: Every Freemason, even if unaffiliated, is subject to the government of the fraternity and can be tried and punished by any of the lodges of the jurisdiction (...) Article 18 of the duties of the Freemasons are (...) 2.- Obey the laws of the country 3.- Consecrate the principles of the inviolability of life, the equality of all men before the law, and combat tyranny, intolerance, fanaticism, and superstitions in all their forms (...) Preserve, even at the cost of sacrifices on their part, the harmony and fraternity that must reign among all the members of the great Masonic family and use all the means at their disposal to avoid any harm to the Order, his brothers, or his sympathizers. Brother Oscar Pérez was tried for violation of these articles. Brother (referring to me), you are a political scientist; I am shocked by your attitude and ignorance of a dictatorship. This government is not to my liking, but you and I know that this government (the Maduro regime) is not even similar to that of Pinochet in Chile or Franco in Spain (...). In those dictatorships, there was no freedom of the press, and You know that here you can say and publish what you want; the repression of the opposition guarimbas was not such; it was containment, in another country and especially in the USA at the first guarimbas they would have been repressed with force, with deaths and injuries and detainees imprisoned for at least 15 years. End the date.

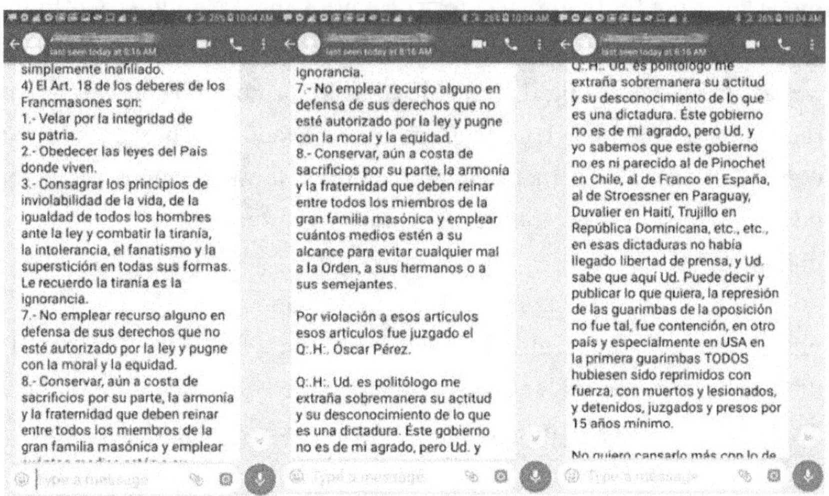

In this message, the public prosecutor acknowledges the trial of Oscar Pérez and what the arguments were.

Perhaps what outrages me the most when reading your argument is the lack of acknowledgment of human rights violations carried out by the Venezuelan state when they were allegedly committed flagrantly before their very eyes, as is the case of the summonses that were issued to five of the members of the Lodge Santiago Mariño Number 208, the names of those affected are Yhonny Calderón, Rubén Rodríguez, Galian Sánchez, Jameson Jiménez and Marcial Jiménez, who were held in the offices of the CICPC -Scientific Police- for more than 11 hours, according to a complaint issued at a press conference by Mrs. Portillo, wife of one of the Masons affected, Jameson Jiménez. But this would be the first outrage against Freemasons committed by the Maduro Regime. The prosecutor speaker's brother was also a witness at the beginning of January 2018 of the kidnapping of Jameson Jiménez and his subsequent arrest after the search by the police and capture of Yhonny Calderón, and he also knew about the third Mason, who had already been arrested in July 2017, it was Ramon Delgado.

I do not understand how the authorities of my Lodge never went to a human rights office to denounce that the Lodge was being affected due to the hunt that the Maduro regime carried out against one of its members.

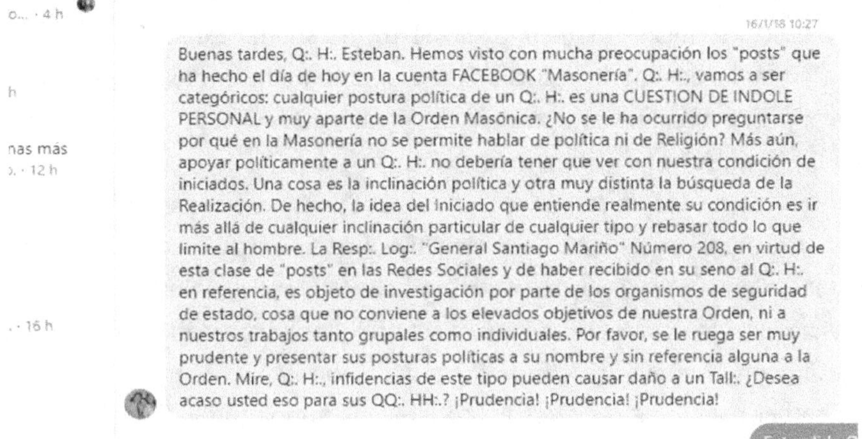

Message from Rubén Rodríguez to Esteban Oria days after the death of Oscar Pérez stating that state security agencies were investigating the lodge.

Tampoco la Gran Logia denuncio estos atropellos. Había suficiente evidencia de violaciones de derechos humanos, debieron haber denunciados ante organismos competentes en el ámbito de los derechos humanos a nivel nacional e internacional, fueron sucesos que ocurrieron en sus logias dentro de los templos, tal como ellos reconocen incluso en un documento, lo cierto fue que la Gran Logia bajo la administración de Jiménez Silva silenció negó estos hechos, encubrieron esta realidad, usaron los medios a su disposición para tergiversar la verdad. Esto se puede constatar en el documento que emitieron con motivo del crimen contra Oscar Pérez, el documento fue firmado por el gran maestro Ubaldo Jiménez Silva y el gran secretario Franklin Barboza.

WHAT THE CONTROVERSIAL DOCUMENT SAYS

Nor did the Grand Lodge denounce these outrages. There was sufficient evidence of human rights violations; they should have denounced them before competent organizations in the field of human rights at the national and international level; they were events that occurred in their lodges inside the temples, as they even acknowledge in a document, what It was true that the Grand Lodge under the administration of Jiménez Silva silently denied these facts, they covered up this reality, they used the means at their disposal to distort the truth. This can be verified in the document issued on the occasion of the crime against Oscar Pérez; the document was signed by the great master Ubaldo Jiménez Silva and the great secretary Franklin Barboza.

On the document's first page, a set of lines are outlined that explain what Freemasonry is; they say that the principles of Freemasonry are mutual tolerance, respect for others and oneself, and absolute freedom of conscience. However, Oscar Pérez's act of conscience received an alleged Masonic prosecution order from them in response.

In another paragraph, they appeal to the constitution of the Grand Lodge; they refer to its article 18 ordinal 2 and 8. I quote, "it is an unavoidable duty to obey the laws of the country where they live and not to use any resource in defense of their rights that is not authorized by the law or conflict with morality and equity." It is clear that in this paragraph, Colonel Jiménez records his loyalty to the Maduro regime:

> Many of the Freemasons, whose particular ideological convictions would make them ascribable to any of these groups, vehemently demand a pronouncement from the GRAND LODGE OF THE REPUBLIC OF VENEZUELA about these events, and they do (some) claiming that it is in accordance with the particulars. Positions (political, religious, social, etc.) that motivate them to claim a pronouncement of this kind: that tends to favor or condemn the actions carried out by the dears brothers, deceased, or by the National Government.

> However, those who aspire to this are ignoring not only the principles that inform the actions of the Venezuelan Freemason institution, to which reference has already been made, but also forget that, according to article 1, first paragraph, of the Constitution of the Grand Lodge of the Republic of Venezuela, in our Order there is no place

for debates on politics and religion. Given that they do not lead to anything other than generating gaps that end »..

Then appears the paragraph of condolences for the relatives, in my opinion, written in the most discourteous way; they refer to dear brother Oscar in the third person, and they seem to mix in the same paragraph condolence with a request to the murderers to take care of investigations of their crimes.

Official and unofficial media that in the end turns out to be accurate, deeply regrets the tragic death of this dears brothers and sends our sincere and heartfelt words of condolence to his relatives for such an unfortunate loss; at the same time that, with due respect, it urges the national authorities so that the events that occurred are investigated, clarified and, if appropriate, the responsibilities that could derive from them are attributed (if it turns out that these deaths were produced by the violation of the norms that regulate procedures such as the one that should have been followed for the apprehension of those who were being the object of any judicial investigation and the consequent violation of human rights); and pray to the G..A.-.D -.U... that circumstances like these never happen again.

After all, we must all aspire and collaborate to maintain the rule of law and guarantee the human rights enshrined in the Constitution of the Bolivarian Republic of Venezuela since they are the foundation of democratic coexistence and peace, as established in article 132 of the Fundamental Charter of the Bolivarian Republic of Venezuela.

Then, in the following paragraph, they waste no time attacking those of us who denounce Maduro and his collaborators. They speak of a person who has denounced that the lodges were raided; according to them, that never happened. This is what the paragraph in question quotes:

Equally obligatory is to point out how some other person has made mentioned in social networks that some Lodges of our jurisdiction would have been "raided" by the military intelligence bodies, a fact that is not true and, from all points of view, Due to this same circumstance, it only tends to worsen the position that, until today, throughout Venezuelan republican and democratic history, the Freemasonic organization had been maintaining with the institutions of the Venezuelan State.

They never found out that the CICPC issued five summonses to members of my lodge Santiago Mariño N 208 for the citizens Rubén Rodríguez, Yhonny Calderón, Jameson Jiménez, Galian Sánchez and Marcial Jiménez, who was detained and interrogated for more than 11 hours, neither they learned that a member of the lodge had been arrested in July 2017 (Ramon Delgado), presented before a military judge and that during his alleged statement-confession he mentioned Freemasonry on at least three occasions, we do not know the reason for the because he did, probably under duress.

These directors of the Venezuelan Freemasonry omitted that in the first days of January 2018, a member of the Mariño lodge was kidnapped by the Maduro collectives; it is Jameson Jiménez; I understand that he was brutally tortured, he was also a headline of the press, neither They were aware that the Maduro regime had issued an arrest warrant against another Freemason from the Santiago Marino lodge, his name Yhonny Calderón, who would later turn himself into the DGCIM and be sentenced for treason.

And continuing with the document, in another of the paragraphs, they contradict themselves again, and on this occasion, they accept the raids.

> In another order of ideas, it must be admitted that it is true that some lodges in the jurisdiction have been visited and the members of their boards of directors invited to appear before the military intelligence agencies.

So they finally acknowledge that the lodges were visited and the members were summoned before military intelligence. It is very serious to admit this chain of events and have done nothing to stop or denounce it.

In the following paragraphs, suppose this was not enough evidence of error after error. In that case, you could read what I interpret as an order to the lodges attached to the Grand Lodge to collaborate with the Maduro police, knowing that the Maduro regime had murdered Oscar Pérez and his group in front of millions of witnesses, committed outrages and crimes against Freemasons assigned to their jurisdiction, but also, the danger that it represented for the Freemasons who are dissidents and opponents of Maduro.

> Faced with these circumstances, it is imposed, as appropriate, to comply with the duties and obligations that the Constitution of the Bolivarian Republic of Venezuela and the laws indicate... When appearing before these bodies, since there is nothing to hide, it is recommended to the representatives of the Lodges to collaborate with the investigation carried out by [the State security bodies, telling the truth about what the objectives pursued and the general principles that inform the universal Freemason institution, the matters that are dealt with in our meeting.-. And, in general, concerning what they deem convenient and always observing (in the terms prescribed by the many times mentioned article 1 of the Constitution of the Grand Lodge of the Republic of Venezuela) the reservation of what corresponds to the Masonic secret that, in accordance with the provisions of article 8 of this internal normative text, refers to the modes of Masonic recognition.

This paragraph puts a lot of people in danger. It is about allowing confessed murderers such as the DGCIM, the SEBIN, or the CICPC to enter the lodges, forcing the brothers to betray each other leaves no doubt of being anti-Masonic, and reaffirms the integrity of my complaint that indicates that they collaborate with organizations accused of violating human rights.

It would be necessary to evaluate and investigate how much this access to information from the Masons contributed to the repressive apparatus of the Maduro police since, in mid-2018, two missing Masons were reported.

A Grand Lodge investigator (Endry Mendez) made the denunciation of the disappeared, who exposed the alleged disappearance of Wilmer Muñoz and Juan Hurtado, both Freemasons attached to the Grand Lodge.

This information was known to the past great teacher Ubaldo Jiménez and the past great secretary Alfredo Tovar because they were the ones who initially requested the investigation and received the results from the investigator. This job cost the investigator risking his life and exile.

The question we ask ourselves is why these authorities of the Grand Lodge, knowing all this information about arrested, persecuted, and disappeared Freemasons, did not go to a human rights office and did not denounce before international instances the abuses that were known.

Finally, the document ends with an appeal to collaboration, to silence what they call discretion, such a slap in the face of intelligence.

Dears brothers. The ones that run are times in which our true affiliation to Freemasonry has been tested, and our actions will clearly demonstrate it... Prudence and temperance must be, now more than ever, the distinctive sign of our way of thinking, speaking andf acting...

It is essential to keep in mind, always, the sense of belonging necessary to ensure the survival of the Order, and this implies, fundamentally, taking into consideration that our actions (all our actions) generate responsibility and that, when this responsibility is capable of embracing For the rest of us, it is necessary to stop and think, even for a minute, to evaluate the scope of the consequences derived from them and, in any case, the advisability of committing to them those who, in themselves, have not been consulted..

susceptible de abrazar a los demás, se impone detenernos a pensar, siquiera un minuto, para evaluar el alcance de las consecuencias derivadas de los mismos y, en todo caso, la conveniencia de comprometer con ellos a quienes, de suyo, no han sido consultados...

En Caracas, a los 26 días del mes de Enero de dos mil dieciocho (2018) de la E∴ V∴.

Juan Ubaldo Jiménez Silva
Muy Respetable Gran Maestro de la Muy Respetable Gran Logia de la República de Venezuela

Franklin Barbosa Suárez
Gran Secretario de la Muy Respetable Gran Logia de la República de Venezuela

Document with the signature of Ubaldo Jiménez Silva and Franklin Barbosa

Next, I will share what the Rome Statute says about crimes against humanity to illustrate the seriousness of what happened in our Order.

Rome Statute Article 7
Crimes against humanity

1. For this Statute, a "crime against humanity" shall be understood as any of the following acts when committed as part of a widespread or systematic attack against a civilian population and with knowledge of the said attack:
a) Murder;
b) Extermination;
e) Imprisonment or other serious deprivation of physical liberty in violation of fundamental norms of international law;
f) Torture;
h) Persecution of a group or collectivity with its own identity based on political, racial, national, ethnic, cultural, religious, or gender reasons defined in paragraph 3, or other reasons universally recognized as unacceptable under international law, in connection with any act mentioned in this paragraph or with any crime within the jurisdiction of the Court;
i) Forced disappearance of persons;
2. For paragraph 1:
e) "Torture" means intentionally causing severe pain or suffering, whether physical or mental, to a person in the defendant's custody or control; however, torture shall not be understood as pain or suffering derived solely from lawful sanctions or that are a normal or fortuitous consequence thereof;
g) "Persecution" shall mean the intentional and serious deprivation of fundamental rights in contravention of international law because of the identity of the group or collectivity;
i) "Forced disappearance of persons" shall mean the apprehension, detention, or kidnapping of persons by a State or a political organization, or with its authorization, support, or acquiescence, followed by the refusal to report on the deprivation of liberty or give information about the fate or whereabouts of those people, to keep them outside the protection of the law for a prolonged period.

CONCEPTS THAT SHOULD BE KNOWN TO ACT WITHIN THE LEGAL FRAMEWORK

The lawyer Verónica Guerrero clarifies two relevant concepts for the witnesses and victims of the Maduro regime to act accordingly under the law.

First, the meaning of lying or hiding information is a crime. In the jurist's opinion, witnesses "in all judicial proceedings are obliged to tell the truth, or what is the same, not lie, and contribute with their testimony to clarify the facts. In this way, they have to narrate what has been lived or known without deceit or deception. This is not only preached as a legal but also a moral duty. I understand that this situation could apply to all those who have remained silent about the police summons, the arrests, the torture, and the disappearance.

Then there is the legal concept that applies to the situation when doing nothing becomes a crime; she argues that "failing to help a person who is in a dangerous case, when it can be done, can lead to, without looking for it, and without having done anything, we find ourselves immersed in criminal proceedings precisely because of that passivity. An example of not doing it was when they left Oscar Pérez alone when he surrendered to Maduro's forces; prosecutors, deputies, and human rights organizations were absent in the act. And is that in that case, we could be charged with a crime of omission of the duty of relief, which can lead to the imposition of fines and even, in the most severe cases, imprisonment.

What is the crime of concealment?

To conceal means to cover or hide something. In a criminal sense, concealment is malicious conduct carried out by a person who, without having participated in a previous crime of which he is aware, helps the perpetrator to evade the action of Justice or to take advantage of the effects of the crime committed.

What actions are punished in the crime of concealment?

The concealer may commit the crime by helping the perpetrators or accomplices to benefit from the crime by concealing, altering, or rendering the crime useless.

So "cover-up" is knowing the commission of a crime (in which no intervention has been made at any time, that is, one is not an accomplice in it) and, at a time after its execution, one intervenes. : helping the perpetrators and accomplices to benefit from the crime, allowing them to prevent the discovery of the criminal act or to evade the police or judicial investigation. Writing a document to twist and misrepresent the truth, manipulate and further expose defenseless people, can be an example of a cover-up.

Complicity facilitates the commission of the crime with its conduct, but it is not decisive for its existence. In most penal codes, the complicity figure is enshrined. It establishes that anyone who contributes to unlawful conduct or provides subsequent assistance by prior or simultaneous agreement is an accomplice.

According to the legal literature, "anyone who knows the commission of a punishable conduct is an accomplice, and without prior agreement, will help to evade the action of the authority or to hinder the corresponding investigation."

In the case of cover-up, a legal interpretation of the ICC says that "for a cover-up crime to be committed, the covered-up act must be within a list of specific crimes: treason, murder of the king or queen, genocide, crime against humanity, crime against people and property protected in case of armed conflict, rebellion, terrorism, homicide, piracy, human trafficking or illegal organ trafficking."

An aggravated case is regulated when the author of the cover-up acts with abuse of public functions. In other words, the concealer must be an authority or public official and help those responsible for a crime.

Regarding hate crimes, it is convenient to share information from the United States Department of Justice. In this sense, The term "hate" can be confusing. When used in the context of hate crime law, the word "hate" does not mean rage, anger, or general displeasure. In this context, "hate" implies a bias against persons or groups with specific characteristics defined by the Law.

At the federal level, hate crime laws include crimes committed based on race, color, religion, national origin, sexual orientation, gender, gender identity, or disability, actual or perceived.

In this sense, it should be noted that the Maduro regime used a method to hunt down Oscar Pérez, including systematic persecution of Freemason members of his lodge, where there was a summons to arrests and torture. New complaints speak of forced disappearances, all Freemasons.

In the ICC, the concept of victims is associated with natural persons who have suffered harm due to the commission of a crime under its jurisdiction, which is mentioned in the Rome treaty to which we have already referred.

According to the ICC, the victims can be direct or indirect.

- Direct victims are those who suffered direct harm due to a crime within the jurisdiction of the ICC.

- Indirect victims are those who suffered harm due to the harm suffered by the direct victim (for example, if the person is a relative of a victim who died or suffered another type of harm due to a crime within the jurisdiction of the ICC).

Organizations or institutions that have suffered direct damage to some of their assets dedicated to religion, education, arts, sciences, or charity, and to their historic monuments, hospitals, and other places or objects you have are also considered victims. Humanitarian purposes.

It is important to note that crimes against humanity do not prescribe; therefore, witnesses and victims must report to the competent bodies, given that they are not subject to being confused as accessories or collaborators.

The persecution of Freemasons in Venezuela is already widely known and has a precedent for international protection. It is known that the French Government, through the National Court for the Right to Asylum, has granted political asylum to the Freemason brother Ángel Fajardo, a member of the Santiago Mariño Lodge No. 208 and related to the unfortunate brother Óscar Pérez.

In the case of Ángel Fajardo, the French Court of the Right to Asylum has inquired into the impact, manner, and consequences of the Maduro regime's persecution of Óscar Pérez and his group of like-minded people and determined that it was sufficient to cause to benefit him with the asylum protection. The asylum cases have been observed and understood by the situation suffered by brother Ángel Fajardo and have received protection under the Geneva Convention of July 28, 1951. This is the first legal precedent for Masons in Venezuela.

The most recent thing is that the office of the International Criminal Court has been aware of these complaints; in this sense, we have integrated a group of Freemasons and created an ad hoc group with the specific objective of making the complaints public, promoting the investigation before the competent bodies.

We have received a response to the receipt of the document that we sent to prosecutor Karim Khan, which is nothing more than a public letter that he published in El Nacional under the title Public letter to prosecutor Karim Khan, Oscar Pérez case and Freemasonry, by Esteban Oria dated January 20, 2022 (https://www.elnacional.com/opinion/carta-publica-al-fiscal-karim-khan-caso-oscar-perez-y-la-masoneria/)

KNOWING THE PAST GRAND MASTER UBALDO JIMÉNEZ SILVA

Finally, it is worth knowing an essential detail about the questioned character who directed the destinies of Freemasonry in the period 2017 - 2018; the past grand master Ubaldo Jiménez Silva is an army colonel who held important positions of trust, including the secretary of the Experimental University of the Armed Forces. The colonel was also involved in a series of trials in the Martial Court and the Supreme Court of Justice.

It is known that the Court Martial in 1999 sentenced Colonel Jiménez to an 11-year prison sentence for the alleged commission of the crimes of theft of funds belonging to the Armed Forces, in a degree of continuity and abuse of authority. Then the Supreme Court of Justices acquitted him of said crimes.

So to understand the context of his decisions, it is essential to highlight this event; I am going to share some extracts of the decisions published on the website of the Supreme Court of Justice page.

> However, in the case brought to the consideration of this Chamber, the order to open a summary investigation against Brigadier General (GN) Ramón Antonio Rodríguez Mayol and Colonel (GN) Juan Ubaldo Jiménez Silva for alleged irregularities presented is verified. Regarding the first, during his tenure as head of the Finance Directorate of the Venezuelan National Guard, the Training School for Officers of the Armed Forces of Cooperation and the Regional Command No. 5 of the National Guard, and the second, during his management as Head of the Administration and Logistics Division of the Command mentioned above, an investigation that warranted the judicial detention of the previous citizens, for the alleged commission of the crimes of theft of funds belonging to the National Armed Forces, in a degree of continuity; illegal payment order through improper receipts, abuse of authority and conspiracy.

Print Copy of the Supreme Court of Justice website about the paper referring to the case where Colonel Jiménez Silva is involved.

COMUNICADO 01

La GRAN LOGIA DE LA REPÚBLICA DE VENEZUELA, luego de mucho reflexionar en relación a los innumerables hechos acontecidos a partir del día lunes 15 del corriente mes de enero de 2018, ha considerado necesario invitar a la población masónica nacional a **VOLVER SOBRE LOS PRINCIPIOS GENERALES** que informan la actuación de la Masonería Universal (sustentados en la práctica de las virtudes: "prudencia", "templanza", "fortaleza" y "justicia") y, con soporte en ellos, efectuar las siguientes reflexiones:

De acuerdo con lo establecido en el artículo 1 de la Constitución de la Gran Logia de la República de Venezuela, norma estatutaria que representa el pináculo del ordenamiento jurídico positivo interno de la masonería regular de nuestro país, la Francmasonería es una institución esencialmente filantrópica y progresiva que tiene por objeto tanto la investigación de la verdad como el estudio y la práctica de la moral y la solidaridad. De modo que, esta es una institución que trabaja arduamente por el mejoramiento espiritual y material de la humanidad, así como también por su perfeccionamiento individual y social.

Dentro del específico ámbito de su concepción eminentemente "filantrópica", la Francmasonería ha procurado siempre (sin esperar nada a cambio) formar cabalmente al hombre para que sea verdaderamente libre y para que, desprovisto de las gruesas cadenas de la ignorancia, el fanatismo y la superstición, con la firmeza de carácter que se requiere, sea capaz de obrar en el mundo profano, **a título personal** (como ser humano, como ciudadano, como padre, como hijo, como esposo, como comerciante, como artesano, como profesional, etc.) atendiendo a los empinados valores que informan la moral y la ética, de modo que se convierta (en su familia, en su entorno, en su comunidad, en la sociedad entera) en un farol de luz cuyo digno ejemplo de esfuerzo, constancia, dedicación, trabajo, progreso, lealtad, honestidad y dignidad sea merecedor de ser replicado y seguido por quienes lo rodean.

Precisamente por ello, la historia patria (así como la historia universal) está llena de ejemplos de insignes personajes que se han destacado notablemente (en los oficios, las tareas, las ciencias y las artes de las más variadas especies que les ha correspondido ejercer) por los enormes beneficios que sus obras han aportado a la sociedad de su tiempo y que, además, en su faceta menos conocida (por no decir desconocida) también eran masones. No en vano, en ese mismo artículo 1 de la Constitución de la Gran Logia de la República de Venezuela, en su cuarto aparte, se postula que la Francmasonería recomienda a sus adeptos hacer propaganda de los principios de esta institución por medio del ejemplo derivado de su conducta cotidiana, observando siempre la reserva del secreto masónico.

Así las cosas, fiel a los principios que la informan (que no son otros que la tolerancia mutua, el respeto a los demás y de sí mismo, y la libertad absoluta de conciencia) la Francmasonería deja en libertad a cada uno de quienes forman parte de ella para atender a los dictados de su propia conciencia y de obrar conforme le indiquen los valores y principios que a lo largo de sus vidas han aprehendido, asumiendo, como ciudadanos, las responsabilidades derivadas de sus propios actos. Y lo hace, porque está consciente de que un masón es, fundamentalmente, y por definición, un hombre virtuoso, amante de su patria y respetuoso de las leyes del país en el que vive.

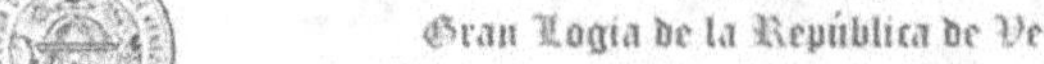

A L∴ G∴ D∴ G∴ A∴ D∴ U∴
Francmasonería Regular Universal – R∴ E∴ A∴ A∴
Familia Venezolana

Gran Logia de la República de Venezuela

Instalada el 24 de Junio de 1824 (e∴ v∴) Constitución 1924 ·Personería Jurídica desde 1944
Miembro de la Confederación de Grandes Logias Regulares del Mundo - Miembro de la Confederación Masónica Interamericana –
Miembro de la Confederación Masónica Bolivariana
Gran Templo Masónico, Jesuitas a Maturín N° 5, Caracas, D.F. Monumento Histórico Nacional
Teléfonos. (02) 6609548 – 8605776 Fax: (02) 660 5776
Apartado de Correos 927 – Caracas 1010-A – Venezuela
Internet: http:// www.granlogia.org.ve

De modo que, la Francmasonería respeta y no interviene de ninguna manera en las decisiones que, ajenas a la institución, a título personal, como individuo perteneciente a un determinado grupo familiar, profesional o social, en definitiva: como ciudadano, haya podido tomar cualquiera de sus integrantes; así como también respeta, no interviene y no toma partido de las acciones que, en ese ámbito, aquel haya podido llegar a ejecutar. Este respeto se encuentra fundado, precisamente, en el hecho de que para todo masón, a tenor de lo establecido en el artículo 18, ordinales 2º y 8º, de la Constitución de la Gran Logia de la República de Venezuela, constituyen deberes insoslayables el "obedecer las leyes del país donde viven" y "no emplear recurso alguno en defensa de sus derechos que no esté autorizado por la ley o pugne con la moral y la equidad".

Sobre la base de lo que se acaba de indicar, bien vale la pena observar que, en los últimos días, la trágica muerte del Q∴H∴ Oscar Pérez ha concitado el pronunciamiento de múltiples y variadas opiniones (en relación a sus actuaciones previas y a la forma en que su deceso se produjo) de los distintos sectores de la sociedad venezolana y la comunidad internacional (algunos afectos al gobierno, otros afectos a la oposición política y otros tantos que no se adscriben a ninguna de estas parcialidades) que, como es lógico suponer, también se ven reflejados de alguna manera entre los integrantes de la masonería venezolana.

Muchos de los masones cuyas convicciones ideológicas particulares los harían adscribibles a cualquiera de estos grupos, reclaman vehementemente un pronunciamiento de la GRAN LOGIA DE LA REPÚBLICA DE VENEZUELA en relación a estos sucesos y lo hacen (algunos) pretendiendo que éste se encuentre acorde con las particulares posiciones (políticas, religiosas, sociales, etc.) que los motivan a reclamar un pronunciamiento de esta especie: que tienda a favorecer o a condenar las acciones llevadas a cabo por el Q∴H∴ fallecido o por el Gobierno Nacional.

Sin embargo, quienes ello aspiran, están pasando por alto no sólo los principios que informan la actuación de la institución francmasónica venezolana, a los que ya se ha hecho referencia, sino que olvidan también que, conforme al artículo 1, primer aparte, de la Constitución de la Gran Logia de la República de Venezuela, **en nuestra Orden no tienen cabida los debates sobre política y religión**, habida cuenta que ellos no conllevan a otra cosa que no sea generar brechas que terminan por alejar y enemistar a quienes son partidarios de tendencias distintas, y esto, de suyo, es contrario al sentimiento de hermandad y fraternidad que priva entre los masones esparcidos por el orbe.

No obstante, enmarcados en el ámbito delineado anteriormente (que implica la tolerancia mutua, el respeto por los demás y la libertad absoluta de conciencia) respetando las opiniones y posiciones que eventualmente, en relación a estos hechos, hayan podido tomar los distintos sectores del país (independientemente de que éstos se vean reflejados o no en la población masónica nacional), la GRAN LOGIA DE LA REPÚBLICA DE VENEZUELA, atendiendo, por una parte, al deber de consagrar los principios de inviolabilidad de la vida y la igualdad de todos los hombres ante la ley, previsto en el artículo 18, ordinal 3º, de la Constitución de la Gran Logia de la República de Venezuela (cuyo reconocimiento y garantía se halla en los artículos 21 y 43 del Texto Fundamental de la República Bolivariana de Venezuela) y, por otra parte, al natural sentimiento de dolor y frustración que se deriva de la pérdida de una vida, sea cual fuere la condición del individuo a quien se le arrebate en las trágicas condiciones en las cuales se verificó deceso del Q∴H∴ Oscar Pérez y el grupo de personas que lo acompañaba, independientemente de la versión de los hechos (ofrecida tanto por

A L∴ G∴ D∴ G∴ A∴D∴ U∴
Francmasonería Regular Universal - R∴ E∴ A∴ A∴
Familia Venezolana

Gran Logia de la República de Venezuela

Instalada el 24 de Junio de 1824 (e∴ v∴) Constitución 1924 -Personería Jurídica desde 1944
Miembro de la Confederación de Grandes Logias Regulares del Mundo - Miembro de la Confederación Masónica Interamericana –
Miembro de la Confederación Masónica Bolivariana
Gran Templo Masónico, Jesuitas a Maturín Nº 5, Caracas, D.F. Monumento Histórico Nacional
Teléfonos: (02) 8609545 – 8605776 Fax: (02) 860 5776
Apartado de Correos 927 – Caracas 1010-A – Venezuela
Internet: http:// www.granlogia.org.ve

los medios oficiales como por los extraoficiales) que a la final resulte ser cierta, **lamenta profundamente el trágico fallecimiento de este Q∴H∴ y hace llegar a sus familiares sus más sinceras y sentidas palabras de condolencia por tan lamentable pérdida**; al propio tiempo que, con el debido respeto, **exhorta a las autoridades nacionales a los fines de que los hechos acaecidos sean investigados, esclarecidos y, de resultar ello procedente, sean atribuidas las responsabilidades que podrían derivarse de los mismos** (de resultar que esas muertes se produjeron por la violación de las normas que regulan procedimientos como el que debió seguirse para la aprehensión de quienes estaban siendo objeto de una investigación jurisdiccional cualquiera y la consiguiente violación de los derechos humanos); y **ruega al G∴A∴D∴U∴ que circunstancias como éstas no se repitan jamás.**

Al fin y al cabo, al mantenimiento del Estado de Derecho y al aseguramiento de los derechos humanos consagrados en la Constitución de la República Bolivariana de Venezuela debemos aspirar y colaborar todos, pues ellos son el fundamento de la convivencia democrática y de la paz social de la nación, tal y como lo establece el artículo 132 de la Carta Fundamental de la República Bolivariana de Venezuela.

Por otra parte, resulta obligante hacer notar la existencia de una insana campaña de desprestigio que (a nivel nacional e internacional) viene desarrollándose en contra de la institución francmasónica venezolana en general y la GRAN LOGIA DE LA REPÚBLICA DE VENEZUELA en particular.

Prueba de ello es que, hace unos pocos días, circuló por las redes sociales un COMUNICADO que habría emanado del Muy Respetable Gran Maestro y el Gran Secretario de la GRAN LOGIA DE LA REPÚBLICA DE VENEZUELA, en el cual se indicaba que el Q∴H∴ Oscar Pérez habría sido expulsado de la masonería por la Alta Cámara de Justicia de la Gran Logia de la República de Venezuela.

Así las cosas, es menester advertir ahora que el aludido COMUNICADO es **ABSOLUTAMENTE FALSO**... Que tal falsedad queda al descubierto al observar que **no es cierto**, desde ninguna perspectiva, **que los órganos disciplinarios de la GRAN LOGIA DE LA REPÚBLICA DE VENEZUELA** (a saber: el Tribunal de la Gran Logia, la Alta Cámara de Justicia y el Tribunal de la Gran Cámara del Simbolismo Nacional) **hayan instruido y mucho menos decidido** procedimiento alguno que guarde relación con causa que tenga como objeto procurar la expulsión de la Orden Francmasónica, por cualquier motivo, al Q∴H∴ Oscar Pérez; que en el instrumento que se hizo circular en las redes sociales (a pesar de estar fechado en enero de 2018) aparecería suscribiéndolo como Gran Secretario, el Q∴H∴ Alfredo Tovar, cuando se sabe que, en realidad, en la Junta Directiva de la GRAN LOGIA DE LA REPÚBLICA DE VENEZUELA, tales funciones son ejercidas por el Q∴H∴ Franklin Barboza; y que, además, las firmas que en el señalado instrumento se aprecian, no son, desde ningún punto de vista, las del Muy Respetable Gran Maestro, la del Q∴H∴ Alfredo Tovar o la del Q∴H∴ Franklin Barboza.

Desafortunadamente, ese instrumento falso no sólo se hizo circular en las redes sociales para generar rumores (a favor o en contra de lo que habría sido decidido) entre los masones venezolanos, sino que, además, se hizo llegar a Grandes Potencias Masónicas del extranjero y, lo que es peor aún, se generó en ellas el convencimiento de que era menester acogerlo para, de alguna manera, a pesar de las advertencias de no pretender inmiscuirse en asuntos propios de la masonería

A L∴ G∴ D∴ G∴ A∴D∴ U∴

Francmasonería Regular Universal – R. E. A. A.
Familia Venezolana

Gran Logia de la República de Venezuela

Instalada el 24 de Junio de 1824 (e∴ v∴) Constitución 1924 -Personería Jurídica desde 1944
Miembro de la Confederación de Grandes Logias Regulares del Mundo - Miembro de la Confederación Masónica Interamericana –
Miembro de la Confederación Masónica Bolivariana
Gran Templo Masónico, Jesuitas a Maturín N° 5, Caracas, D.F. Monumento Histórico Nacional
Teléfonos: (02) 8609548 – 8605776 Fax: (02) 860 5776
Apartado de Correos 927 – Caracas 1010-A – Venezuela
Internet: http:// www.granlogia.org.ve

regular venezolana, con sus pronunciamientos agredir o descalificar de cualquier forma (aunque fuera de soslayo) a la GRAN LOGIA DE LA REPÚBLICA DE VENEZUELA frente a la comunidad (masónica y no masónica) nacional e internacional.

Igualmente obligante es hacer observar como alguno que otro personero ha hecho mención en las redes sociales, que algunas Logias de nuestra jurisdicción habrían sido "allanadas" por los cuerpos de inteligencia militar, hecho éste que **no es cierto** y, desde todo punto de vista, por esa misma circunstancia, tiende sólo a desmejorar la posición que, hasta el día de hoy, a lo largo de lo historia republicana y democrática venezolana, había venido manteniendo la organización francmasónica con las instituciones del Estado Venezolano.

De modo que, hay que decirlo, es importante evitar hacerse eco de comentarios e informaciones (falsas, inexactas y no confirmadas) que, en este clima de crispación imperante, caldo de cultivo perfecto para hacer brotar las pasiones más bajas, sólo conducen a perjudicar la bien ganada buena reputación de la institución francmasónica venezolana y sus integrantes. Y mucho más importante aún es evitar especular en relación a lo que ha acontecido o viene aconteciendo, sin tener conocimiento exacto de ello y sin sacar conclusiones apresuradas (por no decir temerarias) en relación al "prudente silencio" que, hasta el día de hoy, había mantenido la GRAN LOGIA DE LA REPÚBLICA DE VENEZUELA para poder dedicarse a evaluar con detenimiento todos los elementos necesarios para producir una opinión como la que, en este momento, en muy largos términos se profiere.

Al fin y al cabo, constituye un deber indeclinable de todo masón el tener qué conservar la armonía y la fraternidad que deben reinar entre todos los miembros de la gran familia masónica y emplear cuantos medios estén a su alcance para evitar cualquier mal a la Orden, a sus hermanos o a sus semejantes, tal y como lo señala el ordinal 8° del artículo 18 de la Constitución de la Gran Logia de la República de Venezuela.

En otro orden de ideas, hay que admitir que es absolutamente cierto que algunas Logias de nuestra jurisdicción han sido visitadas y los integrantes de sus juntas directivas invitados a comparecer ante los organismos de inteligencia militar.

Frente a estas circunstancias, se impone, tal y como corresponde, cumplir con los deberes y obligaciones que la Constitución de la República Bolivariana de Venezuela y las leyes indican... Al comparecer ante estos cuerpos, siendo que nada hay que esconder, se recomienda a los representantes de las Logias colaborar con la investigación que adelantan los cuerpos de seguridad del Estado diciendo la verdad en relación a lo que son los objetivos que persigue y los principios generales que informan la institución francmasónica universal, las materias que son tratadas en nuestras TTen∴ y, en general, respecto de cuanto estimen conveniente y necesario, observando siempre (en los términos que prescribe el tantas veces mencionado artículo 1 de la Constitución de la Gran Logia de la República de Venezuela) la reserva de lo que corresponda al secreto masónico que, conforme a lo establecido en el artículo 8 de ese texto normativo interno, está referido a los modos de reconocimiento masónico.

Así, pues, siendo un deber de todo masón, a tenor de lo establecido en el artículo 18, ordinal 10°, de la Constitución de la Gran Logia de la República de Venezuela, proteger a sus hermanos en cuanto le

A∴ L∴ G∴ D∴ G∴ A∴D∴ U∴
Francmasonería Regular Universal – R∴ E∴ A∴ A∴
Familia Venezolana

Gran Logia de la República de Venezuela

Instalada el 24 de Junio de 1824 (e∴v∴) Constitución 1924 -Personería Jurídica desde 1944
Miembro de la Confederación de Grandes Logias Regulares del Mundo - Miembro de la Confederación Masónica Interamericana –
Miembro de la Confederación Masónica Bolivariana
Gran Templo Masónico, Jesuitas a Maturín N° 5, Caracas, D.F. Monumento Histórico Nacional
Teléfonos: (02) 8609548 – 8605776 Fax: (02) 860 5776
Apartado de Correos 927 – Caracas 1010-A – Venezuela
Internet: http://www.granlogia.org.ve

permitan sus medios y ello no se oponga a la moral, importa recordar que si bien es cierto que es un derecho de todo masón revelar su condición de tal a quien desee, no es menos cierto que no es permitido, sin embargo, revelar la condición de masón de otro Q∴ H∴ que ha preferido mantenerla en reserva. En consecuencia, esa información, salvo mejor criterio, no puede ser suministrada sino previa la emisión de una orden judicial al respecto que haya sido precedida, claro está, de una sentencia judicial que haya declarado la nulidad del estatuto legal masónico que impone, bajo fe de juramento, el deber de guardar silencio a este respecto.

QQ∴ HH∴ los que corren son tiempos en los cuales se ha puesto a prueba nuestra verdadera afiliación a la Francmasonería y serán nuestras acciones las que darán clara demostración de ello... La prudencia y la templanza han de ser, ahora más que nunca, el *signo distintivo de nuestra forma de pensar*, de nuestra forma hablar y de nuestra manera de actuar...

Es imprescindible tener presente, siempre, el sentido de pertenencia necesario para asegurar la supervivencia de la Orden, y ello implica, fundamentalmente, tomar en consideración que nuestros actos (que todos nuestros actos) generan responsabilidad y que, cuando esta responsabilidad es susceptible de abrazar a los demás, se impone detenernos a pensar, siquiera un minuto, para evaluar el alcance de las consecuencias derivadas de los mismos y, en todo caso, la conveniencia de comprometer con ellos a quienes, de suyo, no han sido consultados...

En Caracas, a los 26 días del mes de Enero de dos mil dieciocho (2018) de la E∴ V∴

Juan Ubaldo Jiménez Silva
Muy Respetable Gran Maestro de la Muy Respetable Gran Logia de
la República de Venezuela

Franklin Barboza Suárez
Gran Secretario de la Muy Respetable Gran Logia de la República de
Venezuela

DETAILS OF THE PERSECUTION OF MASONS AND THE DUTY OF THE MEMBERS OF THE SANTIAGO MARIÑO LODGE 208

July 2017.

In the middle of July, the police summonses began to arrive to the members of the lodge, weeks after Oscar's rebellion occurred; those interrogated were Rubén Rodríguez, Yhonny Calderón, Jameson Jiménez, Galian Sánchez and Marcial Jiménez, these brothers were held against their will for more than 12 hours under intense interrogation at the offices of the CICPC criminal investigation body.

This information became publicly known through a statement to the press offered by Mrs. Portillo, wife of Jameson Jiménez, as a result of Jameson's kidnapping in January 2018. She was accompanied at a said press conference by lawyers from the criminal court, who said back then: "in July 2017, CICPC officials went to my house to take him to give some statements about the Oscar Pérez case; he is a friend of his (Oscar Pérez) since childhood, they detained him from 7 in the tomorrow until 11 at night, a whole day giving statements, nothing else happened, and he was working the next day (...), and the journalists asked him: so he was subjected to interrogation for that case months before? Who had it, what did they say mistreated him, and how long was he held? He was there since seven in the morning; it wasn't just him; it was a group of people from the lodge because he is a Mason". And he closes quotes..

The photo shows some members who were affected by the police summons, top left: Yhonny Calderón, Rubén Rodríguez, bottom left Galián Sánchez.

The arrest of Ramon Delgado

July 2017. I also found out that, at the beginning of July 2017, the regime had arrested a recently initiated lodge member named Ramon Fernando Delgado Vegas; I understand that he was an official of the Public Ministry. Later I found out that he was presented on charges of rebellion and insulting the sentinel, the flag, and the national armed force. The military judge in charge was Claudia Carolina Pérez Mogollón.

Even though the lodge learned of the arrest of this Freemason, we never knew the content of his statement. I came to find out in 2022 because they shared this information with me from Venezuela due to my investigation into the persecution of Freemasons.

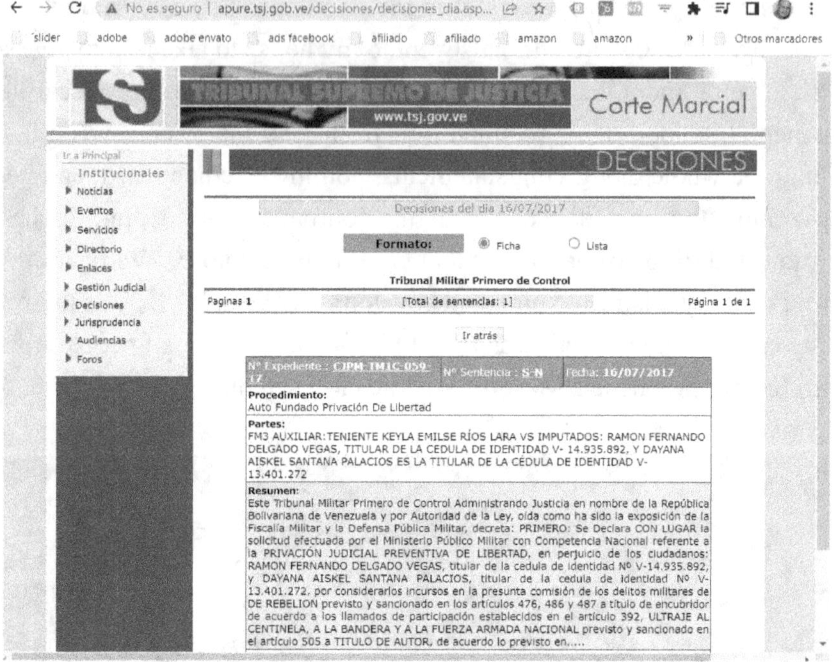

Print copy of the website of the Supreme Court of Justice about the sentence of Ramón Delgado

I know Ramon Delgado was an apprentice Mason member of the Santiago Mariño Lodge Number 208, who supposedly had met with Oscar Pérez in his house days before the uprising.

His statement before the military court that prosecuted him was published on the Supreme Court of Justice website.

When questioned by the judge, Major Claudia Carolina Pérez Mogollón, the alleged defendant Ramón Delgado replied: "I deny the charges against me; I was in Santa Fe, in the house of Oscar Pérez, for the Freemasonry Group. I invite him to a skao group for movie activities; we have been gathering books and ideas we have exchanged to ascend to the next grade. They met on June 25, 2017, in Santa Fe, and he invited me to ride in the helicopter and shoot. That's when I answer him " are you crazy?".

In a recent image posted on Instagram, freemason Ramón Delgado can be seen sitting in what appears to be a court seat in Caracas wearing a Public Defense shirt. One of the functions of the public defense in Venezuela is to assist and represent police officers in administrative and judicial investigations against them, specifically in administrative, contentious-administrative, and criminal jurisdiction.

"Consequently, the citizen Military Judge granted the right to speak to citizen Freddy Jesús Velásquez in his capacity as a private defender of the citizen in order for him to ask the questions that he had to ask the accused citizen and consequently replied: Yes, I wish to ask the defendant questions. Say your relationship with citizen Oscar Pérez? He replied: He had three months of Masonic relationship. Illustrious to the Tribunal on

Freemasonry? He replied: It is for all people's inner being and well-being. What topics are covered there? He replied: We talked about the work that would be done. For what? He replied: With movements to ascend to the higher grade. That's all…"

The court ordered custodial measures for the crime of rebellion. The minutes appear signed on July 16, 2017.

Put in bold the times and ways he used the word Masonry. There is not the slightest doubt that his statement revolved around the order; if you analyze the common thread of the conversation, you could conclude that this information can only be used for Maduro's intelligence for his persecution narrative.

It is possible that this statement was given under duress because it makes no sense to mention Freemasonry in that context, knowing that it meant sending a pack of assassins after us unless it was intentional; I hope that Mr. Delgado gives us his version of the facts and explain the reasons for your statement.

The truth is that, if you calculate the times, it was after that trial and probably no more than two weeks apart that the Maduro regime sent the summons to the members of the Santiago Mariño Lodge Number 208. The harassment and visits began to the lodge.

The kidnapping of Jameson Jimenez
January 2018.

Then there was a period of relative calm that lasted from August 2017 until the first week of January, when Jameson Jiménez was kidnapped. I can say that I knew little about this brother; I saw him with the venerable teacher Rubén Rodríguez, who was very helpful in the affairs of the lodge, taking care of his occupations as an apprentice, I understand that he was in charge of the WhatsApp chats and the issue of the lodge's social networks, we rarely spoke, in short, I found out about his kidnapping through some WhatsApp messages that were shared with me in the group, by then I was already living in the United States.

I learned from press reports that Maduro's colectivos kidnaped Jameson Jiménez on January 4, 2018. He appeared eight days later at one of the National Police headquarters in Caricuao. His wife had reported his disappearance to a criminal forum, what we assume is that a collective group kidnapped him to extract information through torture; we have no idea what kind of torture they applied to him because these operations are outside of official agencies; what are You know what actors like DGCIM or SEBIN do are practices such as beatings, drowning, placing bags of excrement on the head, and rape with an object with anal penetration, among many other forms of torture.

Tweet by Isnardo Bravo @isnardobravo dated 12:09 p.m. m. 7 Jan 2018 "I regret to inform and I say this for his relatives who have been desperately looking for him since last Thursday that the employee of the Ministry of Communication held by the Dgcim is Jameson Jiménez Masa CI 15,208,221"

I learned from press reports that Maduro's colectivos kidnaped Jameson Jiménez on January 4, 2018; he appeared eight days later at one of the National Police headquarters in Caricuao. His wife had reported his disappearance to a criminal forum, what we assume is that a collective group kidnapped him to extract information through torture; we have no idea what kind of torture they applied to him because these operations are outside of official agencies; what are You know what actors like DGCIM or SEBIN do are practices such as beatings, drowning, placing bags of excrement on the head, and rape with an object with anal penetration, among many other forms of torture.

Regarding the type of torture, probably the testimony provided by the brother of the late political scientist colleague Vasco Da Costa can give you an idea of the cruelty practiced by the Maduro regime.

"They beat you; they beat your mouth, eyes, face, ears, and head a lot. After you are injured and all broken, they force the person to defecate,, take the excrement, smear it on your face, ears, and everywhere,y put a leather mask on yo,, andy hang you from that mask until you pass out. When they wake you up, they do it repeatedly..."

Vasco de Gama was released and died of a stroke resulting from a carcinoma in his left eye due to the torture he received.

Returning to the subject of Jameson, after his rescue and two days after the state crime against Oscar Pérez, he decides to leave the country on January 17, 2018, at the Maiquetía International Airport, waiting to board the flight to Spain, to Jiménez. A ban on leaving the country due to an investigation appeared on the migration screen.

Officials from the Military Counterintelligence Directorate (Dgcim) then arrived at the airport and took him away in handcuffs.

On March 12, 2018, Jameson Jiménez was released under restrictive preventive measures because the prosecution did not charge them. At the end of 2019, he was granted asylum in Spain with his entire family.

I selflessly helped this boy; I had the opportunity to chat with his father, and I disclosed his situation on social networks. After his release, we exchanged opinions about brother William Jiménez, something he said did not seem fair to me, and from then on, we no longer have contact.

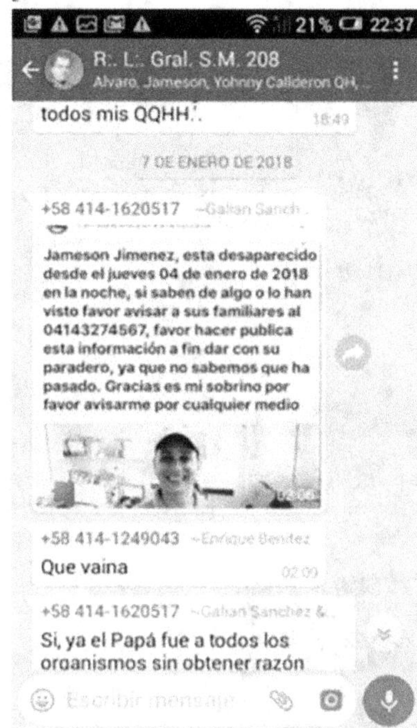

WhatsApp group screenshot.

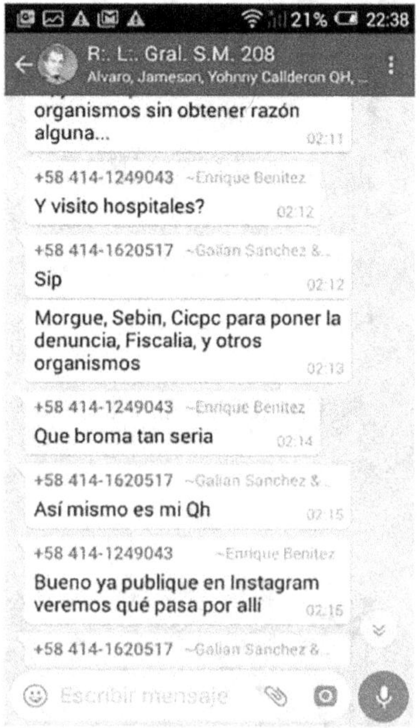

Brothers are concerned about the whereabouts of Jamesón Jiménez..

Home / Destacadas

¡CACERÍA DE BRUJAS! Jameson Jiménez, amigo de Óscar Pérez fue privado de libertad por traición a la Patria

Publicado: 24 enero, 2018 / 9:05 am / Sección: Destacadas, Noticias, Política

El director del Foro Penal Venezolano, Alfredo Romero, denunció que este martes un tribunal militar dictó privativa de libertad **contra un amigo del ex inspector del Cicpc Óscar Pérez.**

Foto: AFP

A través de su cuenta de Twitter, Romero informó que Jameson Marcial Jiménez, quien laboraba en el Ministerio de Comunicación e Información (Minci), **había sido secuestrado el pasado 4 de enero** y su esposa había denunciado su desaparición el 11 de enero.

Un día después Jiménez apareció. Según señaló el FAES, **el hombre fue rescatado del** «hampa común».

ÚNETE A NUESTRA COMUNIDAD

f   3.148.369

        1.864.993

        285.561

        79.400

        69.837

        5.448.160

Recibe por correo el mejor resumen de noticias de Venezuela.

Ingresa tu dirección de correo

Suscribirme

Puedes suspender tu suscripción en cualquier momento.

NOTICIAS DESTACADAS

Camilla Fabri exigió a Estados Unidos negociar la excarcelación de Alex Saab y pidió a la ONU "pronunciarse" por la supuesta violación de sus derechos

Maduradas: WITCH HUNT! Jameson Jiménez, a friend of Óscar Pérez was deprived of liberty for treason

Yhonny Calderón, his only crime, according to the Maduro regime, was being Second Warden of the Santiago Mariño lodge.

Now I want to tell what happened to brother Yhonny Calderón, who was the third arrested after Ramón Delgado and Jameson Jiménez.

Tweet by Alfredo Romero: #26M Political Prisoner released today by Vanessa Barroso, Johnny Calderón, and two others. Congratulations, great family @ForoPenal @MaferTorresA Mariana Ortega Luis Medina, Mariela Suarez

Yhonny Calderón is the only one of those arrested who is part of the old guard; I know him, and he has never had political disputes that I know of; in the first days of January, the Maduro regime requested his capture, his house was raided, he was on the run until after Maduro committed the state crime against Oscar Pérez. He became the Maduro regime; his only crime was being a second guard at the Santiago Mariño lodge number 208.

As second Warden of the Lodge, he was in charge of the Masonic education of Oscar Pérez and José Díaz Pimentel; I suspect that was the reason for his arrest. Yhonny was brought before the courts, and they declared him a traitor to the country, military rebellion, and theft of effects belonging to the armed forces. After spending a year in prison, his case was dismissed on May 29, 2019.

Maduro's intelligence took the time to investigate the position of Yhonny Calderón in the lodge; he was the official in charge of educating the apprentices; the second watchman is like the mentor of the apprentices, surely, Maduro's intelligence was helped by some connoisseur of Freemasonry or a Freemason, and they thought that due to the position he had had something to do with the decisions that Oscar made, the truth is It is that a second watchman does not address political or religious aspects with the apprentices, he dedicates himself more to Masonic symbolism and ritualism. He is currently in exile.

I spoke recently with him by phone; I welcomed him to free land, I also told him about the need for his testimony to be known by public opinion, and I made my opinion column available to him, and I also invited him to fill out and send the consultation form for the opinions and observations of the victims on resuming the investigation in the Situation of Venezuela I before the International Criminal Court, their testimony is very important for the cause of the just, just like the rest of the victims, I think If they all dare to speak and tell their story, we will pave the way to strengthen the pending criminal cases and bring those responsible before the courts of international justice understood in the ICC.

News covering the release of Yhonny Calderon

Galian Sanchez is a witness to the facts
January 2018.

Regarding brother Galián Sánchez, he was one of those summoned by the CICPC police; later, I understood that he was in exile, and now he is in Venezuela; I think that his statement may be of interest to the competent rights organizations humans, I was able to have short conversations with this brother, I hope he takes courage and denounces the abuses committed against him before a human rights organization.

Marcial Jiménez can contribute to the ICC investigation.

January 2018.

Another important testimony for human rights organizations is that of Marcial Jiménez; he experienced firsthand the persecution of his son Jameson Jiménez; he was able to observe the persecution of Maduro against masons from his lodge; he also witnessed the action of the Grand Master Ubaldo Jiménez Silva, at the time I met him remotely, I had the opportunity to talk with him via Chat, I hope that he is one of those who fill out the form of the International Criminal Court to denounce the Maduro regime for what What did.

Rubén Rodríguez has a path to redemption
July 2017.

Finally, there is brother Rubén Rodríguez, who was the venerable master of the lodge; he was also one of those affected by the police summons; he was entrusted to carry out the non-affiliation of Oscar Pérez through the Masonic trial; he told me that The Grand Prosecutor instructed him, I hope that one day he will take courage and reveal who forced him to do this questionable event.

I believe that Rubén made decisions that negatively affected all the members of the lodge; it seems to me he blindly obeyed orders from these authorities of the Grand Lodge, in particular from the Grand Master Ubaldo Jiménez Silva; I only hope for his redemption and to see him one day declare before a human rights instance and even in the International Criminal Court denouncing Maduro for the crimes he committed against his brothers Oscar Pérez and José Pimentel, for the ill-treatment that Maduro's security agencies inflicted on five members of his workshop, including him, for the arrests of three members of his workshop, for the torture of two members of his workshop, and the exile of at least two members of his workshop; I hope you find peace in his conscience.

WHAT I THINK THE WITNESSES AND VICTIMS OF THE SANTIAGO MARIÑO LODGE NUMBER 208 SHOULD DO

All the Freemasons who were summoned to the police, harassed, and besieged for 11 hours, those who were arrested and sentenced in military courts, who later received the benefit of freedom once Maduro executed Oscar Pérez and Díaz Pimentel, these brothers have the moral duty to denounce the Maduro regime for violating human rights, they must do so even before the International Criminal Court and competent human rights organizations, they must denounce the extrajudicial executions that the Maduro regime committed against their brothers Oscar Pérez and José Pimentel.

They must fill out the Victim Consultation form to evacuate their complaints and send them to the International Criminal Court under the designation of victim granted by the ICC. Some of the lodge members meet the conditions to be considered victims or witnesses; then, I share the criteria of the ICC.

In the ICC, the victims are natural persons who have suffered harm due to the commission of a crime under its jurisdiction.

The victims can be direct or indirect.

- Direct victims are those who suffered direct harm due to a crime within the jurisdiction of the ICC.

- Indirect victims are those who suffered harm due to the harm suffered by the direct victim (for example, if the person is a relative of a victim who died or suffered another type of harm due to a crime within the jurisdiction of the ICC).

Organizations or institutions that have suffered direct damage to some of their assets dedicated to religion, education, arts, sciences, or charity, and to their historic monuments, hospitals, and other places or objects that you have are also considered victims. Humanitarian purposes.

Press headline of the news portal Dólar Today: WITHOUT PRECEDENT IN HISTORY; Maduro regime raided Masonic lodges in 6 Venezuelan states

CHAIN OF COMMAND IN THE PERSECUTION OF MASONS

Sources have told me that Maduro, under the advice of Cubans, commissioned General Dala to create a special operation to persecute dissident Freemasons linked to Oscar Pérez.

It is mentioned that the Cuban ambassador to Venezuela, Rogelio Polanco, and the Venezuelan Freemason Freddy Bernal were present at the meeting. It was they who planted the idea that there was a Freemason conspiracy behind the uprising of Oscar Pérez, so Maduro entrusted the mission of dismantling this supposed conspiracy to General Iván Hernández Dala.

What is known as the witch hunt against Masons resulted in a raid on the Santiago Mariño lodge number 208, a Masonic trial against Oscar Pérez, police summonses for five members of the Santiago Mariño lodge number 208, a kidnapping, three arrests, and two forced disappearances, in addition to the extrajudicial executions of Oscar Pérez and José Pimentel. Next, the alleged chain of command behind the so-called Witch Hunt against Freemasons is presented.

CHAIN OF COMMAND

Nicholas Maduro. Higher command of the pursuit operation:

General Iván Hernández Dala, Directorate of Military Intelligence DGCIM. Coordinator of the Operation against the freemasons related to Oscar Pérez.

General Iván Darío Hernández Dala, director of Military Counterintelligence

Particular cases

Case 1

The raiding of lodges, police summons of the Masons, Jhonny Calderón, Rubén Rodríguez, Galian Sánchez, Jameson Jiménez, and Marcial Jiménez	Presumed responsible, Commissioner Douglas Rico

Case 2

The arrest of the Freemason Ramon Delgado	Presumed responsible, DGCIM, Alexander Gramko. Executing Judge of the Sentence Military Judge, Claudia Carolina Pérez De Mogollón

Case 3

The kidnapping of Jameson Jimenez.	Presumed perpetrators DGCIM and FAES Captain Jeanpier de Jesús Soto, Captain Blanco

Case 4

The arrest of Freemason Jhony Calderón	Presumed perpetrators Capture Commissioner Douglas Rico

Caso 5

The forced disappearance of the Freemasons Wilmer Muñoz and Juan Hurtado	Presumed responsible, DGCIM and SEBIN. CICPC cover-up

Caso 6

The forced disappearance of the Freemasons Wilmer Muñoz and Juan Hurtado	Presumed responsible, DGCIM and SEBIN. CICPC cover-up

TC   Noticias   +Vistos   A Fondo   Lo Nuestro   Opinión   Migrantes   De interés ·   Multimedia ·   Nosotros ·

Masonería venezolana denuncia "cacería de brujas" tras la muerte de Óscar Pérez

Luisa Quintero | Enero 19, 2018

La iniciación de Pérez en la masonería fue hace cinco años en la Logia Libertadores de Guayana 2, y estuvo a cargo del Gran Maestro Rafael Arturo Carvajal

Las vinculaciones del exinspector del Cicpc Óscar Pérez con las masonería en Venezuela ha desatado una "cacería de brujas" dentro de sus filas para dar con el paradero de posibles cómplices del piloto, que fue asesinado el 15 de enero en un operativo realizado en El Junquito (Distrito Capital) por fuerzas de seguridad del Estado para capturarlo.

Así lo denunció Eliezer González, gran maestro adjunto de la Logia Suroriental de los Antiguos Libres Aceptados, quien explicó el origen masónico de Pérez en Guayana, y condenó los allanamientos de la Dirección General de Contrainteligencia Militar (Dgcim) en otras logias de Venezuela a raíz del exfuncionario.

Noticias relacionadas

Instituto Casla: Dgcim tiene todo un sistema de «espías» en el país con permiso de Maduro

Cuerpos de seguridad mantienen alerta en Las Tejerías tras enfrentarse a delincuentes

Dgcim allana vivienda de la presidenta y la segunda vicepresidenta de la AN-2015

Fiscalía de Perú investigará torturas contra capitán venezolano Luis de la Sotta

Frente Institucional Militar exige la liberación de los presos políticos

Noticias recientes

A 10 años de la muerte de Chávez, Maduro llama a renovar el "compromiso patriótico"

Continúa labor de búsqueda de buzo desaparecido en Anzoátegui

***Diary As Is**. Luisa Quintero|January 19, 2018, Venezuelan Freemasonry denounces "witch hunt" after the death of Óscar Pérez*

HOW I CAME TO EXILE

To locate the moment of my exile, I will resume the chronological order of Maduro's actions against our lodge. The regime had begun its persecution precisely in July with the arrival of the police summons; I was concerned that I was the next to be summoned due to my position as an opponent; keep in mind that I am a columnist for El Nacional, president of the Federation Venezolana de Politólogos, an opposition official from the National Assembly, even though he had no connection to Oscar's movement, he already had a lot to lose from the outset if Maduro's intelligence managed to place me on the scene and incriminate me, and this was something that he did not want to happen, precisely in that framework of situations where it was not known for sure what was behind it, with him the Masonic trial and the interference of Colonel Ubaldo Jiménez from the great mastery.

Like my brothers, I was worried about being in the same camp as Oscar Pérez, who had become public enemy number 1 of the Maduro regime. You didn't have to be very intelligent to suspect what the next steps of the Maduro regime would be with the Freemasons, so I put everything in perspective; I calculated my chances of getting out of this unscathed with my family; that's how I decided to leave Venezuela. I remember that I bought the plane ticket on August 1, 2017, at the LIDO shopping center; there were two tickets to the United States departing on August 18.

From August 1 until my departure, I was practically in hiding, I attended graduate classes at the university, but I refrained from visiting friends and relatives, including my parents; the idea was not to expose them to the hunting of Maduro's agents.

Particularly, this situation of Oscar Pérez generated an unusual alert in me; there was a lot of secrecy; I was completely blind and did not know what the true magnitude of the problem was; as I had previously commented in this book, I did not know that the Freemason Delgado had been interrogated and He had allegedly involved us in his statement, but what did cause me concern was what the regime would do with the WhatsApp Lodge group chat because it was the known problem since all our phones were on that group list. Maduro has been known to use chat conversations as evidence for legal setups in his impeachment trials, all of which constituted enough danger signs.

In the end, between the police summons, the decisions that Rubén made of the Masonic trial, the visits and inquiries of the police to the lodge, the uncertainty about what would happen next, and my situation in the National Assembly with the threats of the collectives, In short, the sum of all these factors led me to a state of alert where I had no other option than to leave Venezuela, harboring the hope that it would be temporary and that I would return to the country when everything calmed down.

I felt great relief when we landed on American soil; I remember that in Miami, we were received by a dear brother who was also my student for the social media management diploma. After a three-hour break, we continue our journey to Atlanta, Georgia.

Esteban Oria received it at the Miami airport.

I kept in touch with the Lodge's WhatsApp group during the months we were in Atlanta. That was how I was able to follow up on events; in fact, I observed the return of a certain level of calm after the police summonses in July and early August.

If my memory serves me correctly, I remember that I had a return date for September 2017, but a week before the scheduled flight departure, I contacted a brother who was well informed by his connections with the regime; I asked him for his opinion on the convenience of our return to the country, he told me that it was best to extend the return as long as possible and even evaluate the possibility of staying because the situation was complicated, I will always appreciate your honesty with me, consult with my family, it was a difficult decision, I decided to take my brother's advice and change the return date to February 2018.

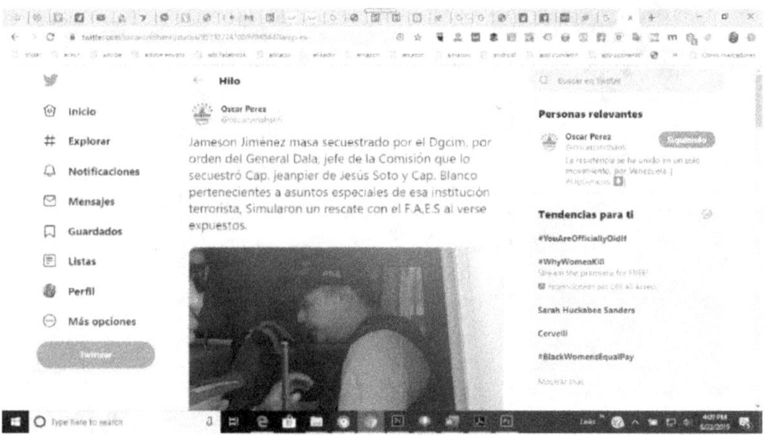

Oscar Pérez Denounces General Hernández Dala on his Twitter account for allegedly kidnapping Jameson Jiménez.

The first days of January struck down my desire to return to Venezuela; it was on January 4, 2018, that I woke up reading help messages on the WhatsApp chat of the lodge; the brothers reported that they had kidnapped Jameson Jiménez, but that they had also had issued an arrest warrant against Yhonny Calderón, both members of the lodge, everyone in the group had panicked, some members of the lodge had visited hospitals looking for Jameson and could not find him, it had been reported that Yhonny had gone to the hiding, he was on the run.

Then on January 11, the Maduro regime, in an alleged operation by its FAES Special Action Forces, reported that they had rescued Jameson; the truth was, it was all a setup; the groups carried out the kidnapping operation at the service of the Maduro regime; I understand that those people were responsible for brutally torturing Jameson.

Print a screen copy of the messages for reasons of the disappearance of Jameson Jiménez and the escape of Yhonny Calderón.

Events happened so quickly that on January 15, 2018, 4 days after Jameson's release, the Maduro regime found the refuge of Oscar Pérez and his group. They were tracked to a chalet in El Junquito, a populous and mountainous parish in Caracas. The house was surrounded by more than 500 officials at the service of Maduro, including armored vehicles, helicopters, national guards, special forces, and colectivos (paramilitaries).

Oscar was broadcasting the siege of his refuge live through social networks; he could transmit all the events live by video on social networks, including his surrender; the evidence was recorded to leave no doubt that what Maduro did was an extrajudicial execution, a state crime.

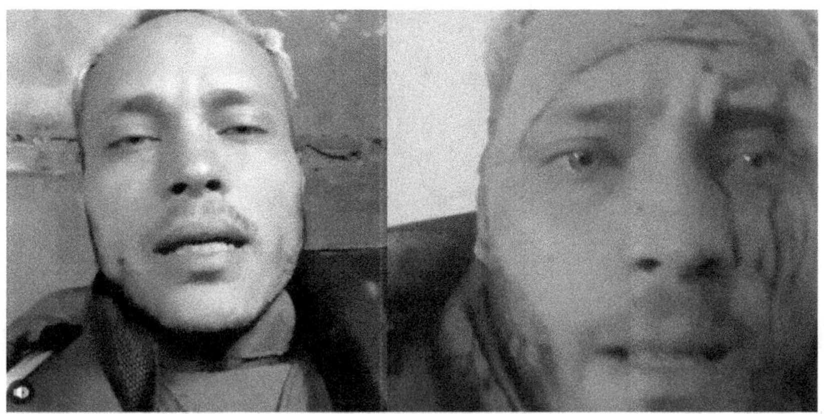

Oscar Pérez broadcasting the assault on his refuge by Maduro officials minutes before he had denounced that Maduro had ordered their assassination.

What happened was that Maduro gave the order to assassinate him, even though Oscar Pérez had surrendered; even the regime did not care about committing this crime, with millions of witnesses following the course of events on social networks.

Maduro, after executing them, with audacity and cynicism, appeared from the podium of the Chamber of Deputies of the National Assembly in a speech broadcast on national television and radio to congratulate the military in charge of perpetrating these homicides; it was about the Minister of the Interior, General Néstor Luis Reverol, the Director of Military Counterintelligence, General Iván Rafael Hernández Dala, and the Defense Minister Padrino López.

I was following this story on my phone in a basement in Schuyler, a small town in Nebraska. I could not believe the degree of impunity prevailing in Venezuela; they had exterminated Oscar Pérez and José Díaz Pimentel before the eyes of millions; both were members of my lodge, people whom I met; I was in shock; they had been murdered in cold blood in front of from the gaze of the whole world, nobody did or said anything, I was not left astonished.

Images that capture the state of the crime scene after the assault at Oscar Pérez's shelter.

"The regime had superiority in firepower, in location (because they surrounded), superiority in mobile equipment, and advantage in the use of large-caliber weapons that was unnecessary for this type of operation (...) the launch of rockets are intended to combat war tanks, and with the distance in which it was launched it indicates the intention of wanting to end the lives of these people"; he explained him.

"Yesterday, the military regulation that speaks of the use of firearms and weapons of war was violated, bearing in mind that these people announced that they would not attack (...) Maduro violated it from the Constitution of Venezuela, where respect for life is established, the Code of Military Justice, the national police law, and even international regulations to the point of having committed a war crime,»; he pointed out.

"He also denounced that after the crime, the regime sought to eliminate the house to hide what happened: "the demolition of the crime scene is yet another violation; it is another element of the regime's guilt since they erased the evidence of an act that should have submitted to investigation.

Was violated the due process of all police and judicial investigation"; denounced."

"The main person responsible is the head of the regime; the one who should have given the order to proceed with the use of a very high caliber weapon should have been Nicolás Maduro, who is the President of the Republic and the Commander-in-Chief of the Venezuelan Armed Forces (...) everyone who has participated has full responsibility to be prosecuted for crimes of violation of human rights, crimes against humanity and war crimes"; he concluded.

When I found out about Oscar's death, I had mixed feelings of impotence, anger, and anxiety; I always held out hope that he would get out alive and that the regime would respect the negotiation, but like many Venezuelans, we were naive.

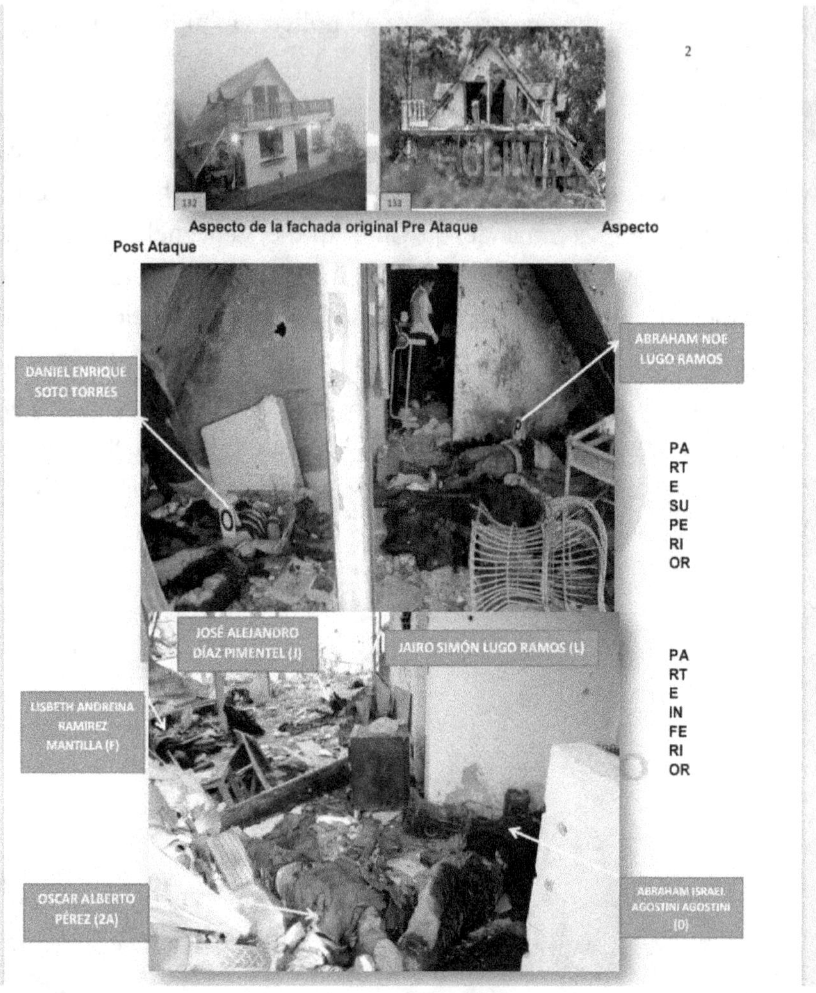

Images taken from the report delivered by former prosecutor Ortega to the ICC show the state of Oscar Pérez's refuge house and his group after being hit by an RPG 7 missile.

After the murder of the brother's Oscar Pérez and José Pimentel, I decided to stay in the United States. My life was in danger in Venezuela, and immediately after these crimes, I contacted the Masonic authorities at the continental level to tell them the story. Of Oscar Pérez's connection with the lodge, I also made public the complaints of persecution of Freemasons by the Maduro regime; I finally decided to stay in the United States and request political asylum, over time I would reactivate my column in El Nacional and deepen the investigations regarding the Oscar Pérez case linked to the freemasons, that is how the complaints of the brothers William Jiménez about the chain of command behind Oscar's crime and those of brother Endry Méndez about the disappearance of the freemasons Wilmer Muñoz and Juan Hurtado arrived. All these complaints are processed and published in my column in the newspaper El Nacional.

THE JUNQUITO MASSACRE

Dear reader, I will make a brief paragraph in this reading to update you on the events that occurred in El Junquito, where Oscar Pérez was assassinated.

The short story was presented in June 2017 with Oscar Pérez transmitting and sharing his video where he is seen rebelling against the regime together with a group of armed men, demanding Maduro's resignation and inviting the people to take advantage of article 350 of the constitution that Quote: "It will disregard any regime, legislation or authority that goes against democratic values, principles, and guarantees or undermines human rights."

What happened after Oscar's uprising was that the video went viral on social networks and news outlets around the world, turning him into an international public figure, he quickly acquired the complexion of a public celebrity, but he also began to be perceived as a new Venezuelan opposition leader.

Oscar's speech was broadcast worldwide; he was especially attractive to youth, who saw him as the incarnation of the leader they expected. Oscar showed himself as a relevant leader who did not fear Maduro; he was also critical of corruption in the opposition. In this way, he galvanized his growing social support.

Although all the police were seeking him, Maduro had put a price on his head; Oscar Pérez could move in the street, making lightning and shocking appearances amid people, causing a great sensation; all those scenes were captured by the media that were later amplified in the press. All the journalists wanted to interview him.

Oscar was consistently forming the image of a Venezuelan hero fighting against the villain of Maduro, whom the German media called "the butcher" for the massacre committed against hundreds of protesters during the 2017 protests.

Oscar Pérez made two incursions into the regime's police posts, subdued the officials, sat them down in front of a camera, and recorded himself giving them classes on human rights and democracy, then published it on social networks, practically making Maduro look ridiculous.

Memes in the networks spoke of the courage of Oscar Pérez

Oscar's strategy sought to raise awareness among the people so they would lose their fear of Maduro, thus creating a critical mass to mobilize millions of citizens to Miraflores.

They were like this for a while, the world followed his exploits with interest, but something happened in those first days of January, and the regime managed to find the whereabouts of Oscar Pérez. Something went wrong in their security ring, I can conjecture, and several ideas come to mind, as do some experts; perhaps a communication failure allowed them to be intercepted and located; I also share the opinion of those who say that someone from their circle betrayed them, in short, only Maduro knows this because in those days they did everything unthinkable to destabilize security and get Oscar out, all this strategy of putting pressure on friends, family, and Masonic brothers was precise to generate pressure upstream towards Oscar.

Mayor Bastardo Mendoza, director of FAES and c Alexander Enrique Granko Arteaga, DGCIM, officials responsible for the extermination operation against Oscar Pérez and his group

Once they located him, Maduro's security forces surrounded him with more than 500 officials; two agents were decisive in that operation against Oscar's group; it was then Major Bastardo Mendoza, director of FAES and now Lieutenant Colonel Alexander Enrique Granko Arteaga, director of Special Affairs of the General Directorate of Military Counterintelligence (DGCIM).

Once he feels surrounded, Oscar activates himself on social networks and denounces that Maduro has ordered his assassination; that is when the older Bastardo appears on the scene, approaches him, and promises a negotiated solution; the conversation is recorded and posted on the networks, What Bastardo tells Oscar is that he has orders from Maduro, that if they turn themselves in they will let them live, you can hear him say the phrase "win-win," that's when Oscar Pérez and his group decide to turn themselves in. Without any explanation, Bastardo leaves the scene, and the shooting begins; they even launch an rpg7 missile against the house's facade where Oscar is taking refuge.

A chronicle from the New York Time newspaper narrates part of the events in detail and comments on the press release that "in a short video that he shared on his Instagram account, we see a bloody and perplexed Pérez: his eyes look nervously at all corners from the room, and the shots make his voice inaudible. He says the authorities ignore his attempts to turn himself in and attack the house with grenade launchers. One video we estimate is from 9:07 am. m. shows one such attack, the second of several, while Pérez and his comrades claimed they wanted to turn themselves into the authorities."

The story continues, "in a video recorded less than an hour later, Pérez, in a panic, shouts his last words amidst the overwhelming fire: "We are going to turn ourselves in! Don't keep shooting!"

The truth is that once the house was hit, the entire façade was destroyed, and the regime's security forces entered, although there were stunned people inside; survivors, it is known that they were executed with coups de grace. Hours later, Maduro announced on a national television network that they had discharged what is a euphemism for not saying Oscar Pérez and his group had been murdered.

The case of brother Oscar Pérez and his group is currently being investigated as a crime against humanity by the ICC. Maduro officials extrajudicially executed each of the members of Oscar's group; they died with coups de grâce and at point-blank range, has been made up of revelations from the report delivered by prosecutor Luisa Ortega Diaz to the International Criminal Court Prosecutor's Office.

About the report, I can tell you that I read it in its entirety; it was given to me by the lawyer and Freemason William Jiménez, who authorized me to disclose it. It was learned that among the victims was a woman who accompanied the group; it is suspected that she was pregnant.

← **Tweet**

Diego E. Arria ✔
@Diego_Arria

.Oscar Pérez.Mártir y héroe d la resistencia y sus 6 compañeros. masacrados x narco tiranía criminal.Pruebas q mañana presenta en CortePenal Int el diputado Wilmer Azuaje. @vladimirpadrino co-responsable.Q dolor.Lean historia

6:44 p. m. · 7 dic. 2019

8.042 Retweets   **328** Tweets citados   **6.851** Me gusta

Tweet Diego E. Arria @Diego_Arria: Oscar Pérez. Martyr, and hero of the resistance and his six companions. Massacred x narco criminal tyranny. Evidence that Deputy Wilmer Azuaje presents in the Int Penal Court tomorrow

LA EJECUCIÓN DEL REBELDE ÓSCAR PÉREZ Y LOS SEIS*

*CUATRO MILITARES, UN PERIODISTA Y UNA ENFERMERA EMBARAZADA

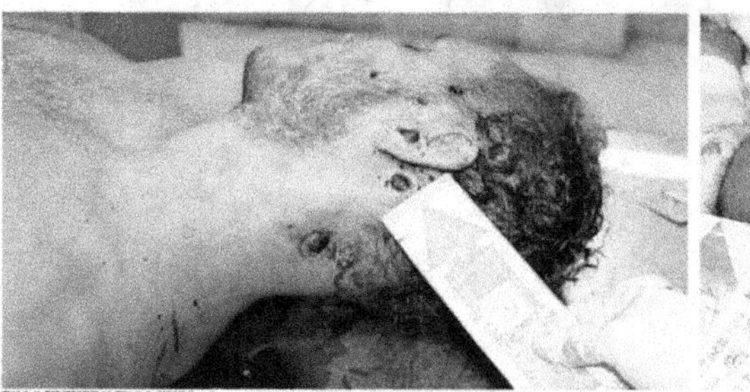

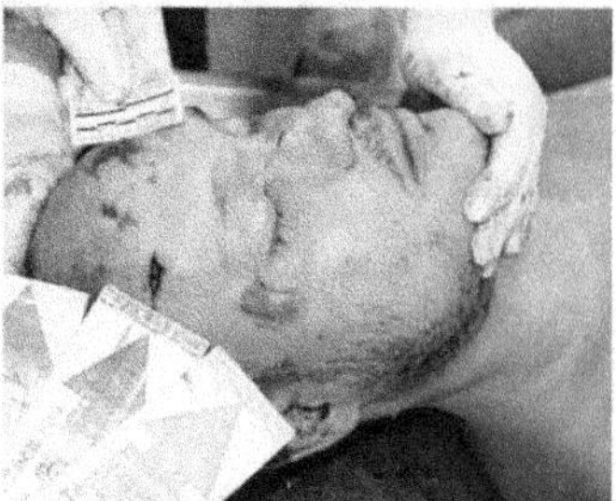

EN LA FRENTE Y EN LA NUCA. Óscar Pérez retratado en la sala de autopsia. Él y su equipo fueron «liquidados», denuncia la fiscal rebelde, Luisa Ortega. IMÁGENES EXCLUSIVAS DE CRÓNICA / EL MUNDO

POR DANIEL LOZANO BOGOTÁ

«El temor a perder la vida es lo menos que tengo ahora. No es el temor de la vida, sino el temor a fracasar, el temor de fallar a la gente». Pocos días después de confesar a *The New York Times* sus inquietudes, como si se tratara de un epitafio a punto de redactarse, el policía rebelde Óscar Pérez y sus seis compañeros de lucha fueron ejecutados por fuerzas gubernamentales en Caracas. De nada sirvió su rendición previa, ni siquiera la negociación con un jefe militar a través de las «ventanas» de las redes sociales. Tampoco las reiteradas súplicas para entregarse: varios horas de asedio y el bombardeo con lanzagranadas a la vivienda donde se refugiaban en El Junquito, a las afueras de la ciudad, precedieron al ametrallamiento final.

Decenas de tiros de gracia para acabar con la vida del famoso *Rambo* venezolano y de su equipo, como llamaba a los seis «libertadores» que se atrevieron a desafiar al todopoderoso chavismo. En su sueño libertario habían anunciado 4 días antes la captura de los poderosos de la revolución para entregarlos a tribunales internacionales. Su cruzada imposible los llevó a la muerte.

Pocas zonas oscuras quedan de lo ocurrido aquel 15 de enero de 2018 a los «mártires de El Junquito». Ninguno se defendió, su única protección fue una bandera blanca que no se respetó y que se tiñó con la sangre de todos ellos. Un capítulo más en la tragedia sin epílogo.

El ex diputado Wilmer Azuaje, quien permaneció más de 400 días en las mazmorras de la Policía política de la capital venezolana pese a disponer de inmunidad parlamentaria, presenta mañana ante la Corte Penal Internacional (CPI) de La Haya una nueva batería de pruebas para demostrar que al grupo del policía Óscar Pérez lo masacraron sin compasión en la casa donde se escondían. Los nombres de quienes acompañaban al piloto de helicóptero más famoso del país ya forman parte de la leyenda antichavista: el funcionario de Contrainteligencia Militar José Alejandro Díaz Pimentel; el militar Abraham Agostini; el

Images published in the Spanish newspaper El Mundo proving that the crime against Oscar and his group was an extrajudicial execution

WHEN FLEEING VENEZUELA BECOMES A QUESTION OF LIFE OR DEATH

periodista Daniel Soto; los hermanos Jairo y Abraham Lugo, ambos guardias nacionales, y la enfermera Lisbeth Ramírez, novia de uno de los hermanos y embarazada de varios meses.

«Voy a entregar más de un centenar de fotografías que confirman que se trata de una ejecución extrajudicial. Se trata de dos causas separadas: la mía, por la violación de mis derechos humanos en 2017 durante mi secuestro en el Helicoide [siniestra sede de la Policía política], y la de Óscar Pérez y los suyos. Cuento con el aval de su madre, Aminta Pérez, y de uno de sus familiares más cercanos, que acudirá conmigo a La Haya», precisó el ex diputado a *Crónica*.

Azuaje, por motivos de seguridad, esconde el nombre de su acompañante. No es para menos. Amigos, compañeros, conocidos o simples simpatizantes de Óscar Pérez son perseguidos desde entonces por las fuerzas gubernamentales, que mantienen entre rejas y entre torturas a varios de ellos.

Hasta el sacerdote que ofició el entierro a la fuerza del *Rambo venezolano*, supervisado por el Gobierno, tuvo que huir del país por las amenazas. Hasta la mujer que alimentó a los perros de Pérez fue detenida en una persecución sin fin. Sobre todos ellos pesa el estigma de la rebelión contra el Estado.

El dirigente opositor y su acompañante cumplirán así el deseo de Aminta Pérez, cuyo salud se quebranto de tanto dolor: «Entregar las pruebas a La Haya, esa va a ser mi misión. Y lograr justicia», subrayó la madre al conocer la odisea emprendida por el ex diputado para que sus reclamos de justicia sean escuchados tras fracasar en su país.

Azuaje es natural de Barinas, la cuna de la revolución, incluso militó en el chavismo antes de abandonar sus filas para denunciar por corrupción a la familia del «comandante supremo». En la actualidad, este dirigente de Primero Justicia (partido del ex candidato presidencial Henrique Capriles y de Julio Borges, «canciller» de Juan Guaidó) se encuentra en el exilio.

La viuda del policía Pérez, sus tres hijos y Aminta están asilados en EEUU. Incluso Donald Trump reconoció públicamente su lucha. La intrahistoria de cómo las imágenes de las pruebas forenses y periciales que confirman la ejecución de los siete jóvenes llegaron hasta Azuaje y la familia del líder del grupo sublevado es otra pequeña historia dentro de la gran historia. El dirigente opositor esconde los detalles más trascendentales, pero detrás de la iniciativa surge otro pequeño héroe. Se trata de Sondas Cortez, detective y compañero de Pérez en la Policía Científica.

«Yo tuve acceso al material fotográfico y luego de evaluarlo me percate de que existía una completa violación de los Derechos Humanos. En vista de que en mi país no se respeta el derecho a la verdad, tomé la decisión de trasladar esas evidencias científicas a Colombia para entregárselas al diputado Wilmer Azuaje y que este las eleve a las instancias jurídicas que sean nece-

sarias y se haga justicia», resumió el policía en una grabación audiovisual de sonido deficiente. Cortez se encuentra escondido hoy en un país latinoamericano.

Las imágenes, a las que ha accedido este suplemento, mezclan crueldad e impunidad, brutalidad y castigo. La violencia sin límites contra un grupo que, desde que Pérez saltara a los periódicos siete meses antes, jamás mató a nadie. El policía, convertido en actor gracias a sus ojos azules y a su carisma, fue el protagonista años antes de una película sobre la institución, titulada *Muerte suspendida*. Otra vez la sombra de su destino.

Una vida que parecía de ficción y que a la postre se convirtió en uno de sus principales obstáculos, al sembrar dudas sobre el origen y los objetivos de su rebelión. A la postre, un héroe al que pocos creyeron.

Pérez conocía a fondo el arte de la defensa, pero no lo exprimió durante su pulso al Estado: en su vuelo en helicóptero sobre el Tribunal Supremo, portando un mensaje con la palabra «Libertad», sólo lanzó un par de granadas aturdidoras. Su intención era levantar la voz «contra la tiranía» en medio del asalto chavista al Parlamento democrático. Después llegarían sus apariciones por sorpresa en concentraciones masivas o sus vídeos en YouTube.

En el asalto a un pequeño cuartel cerca de Caracas, otra pequeña película de no ficción, sólo impartió doctrina a los soldados presentes, que miraban asustados al hombre más buscado como si se tratara de una aparición. En esos momentos no se sentía Rambo, sino una especie de Robin Hood que soñaba con levantar a su pueblo.

El Parlamento democrático y la fiscal rebelde, Luisa Ortega, adelantaron en sus investigaciones que los siete sublevados contra Maduro sufrieron una ejecución extrajudicial. «Resultaron ajusticiados con disparos en la cabeza. La dictadura asesina obviamente jamás abrió investigación para no inculparse a sí misma», denunció la diputada Delsa Solórzano, al frente de la comisión que estudió la masacre.

La fiscal Ortega fue más allá al incluir en el informe enviado a principios de año a la propia CPI una batería de crímenes de lesa humanidad junto a otras pruebas, fotográficas y de la autopsia. «Irrumpieron en la casa y dispararon ráfagas contra Pérez y los suyos. Algunos presentan incluso orificios en las palmas de la mano y en los brazos; se quisieron proteger ante los disparos. Hasta en la guerra la vida de los rendidos debe ser respetada según el Derecho Internacional Humanitario», explica a *Crónica* Ortega desde su exilio en Bogotá. «Los liquidaron», sentencia quien fuera una estrecha colaboradora de Hugo Chávez, convertida hoy en un martillo constante de denuncia contra los abusos del Gobierno de Maduro.

Estamos ante el caso más emblemático de ejecuciones extrajudiciales, que ya parecen una epidemia en Venezuela. El informe de Michelle Bachelet, Alta Comisionada de las Naciones Unidas para los Derechos Humanos, recogió centenares

de ejemplos, la mayoría protagonizados por las Fuerzas Especiales de la Policía (FAES), «batallones de exterminio» (según la ONU) creados por Maduro en 2017. La ex presidenta socialista de Chile recomendó su disolución.

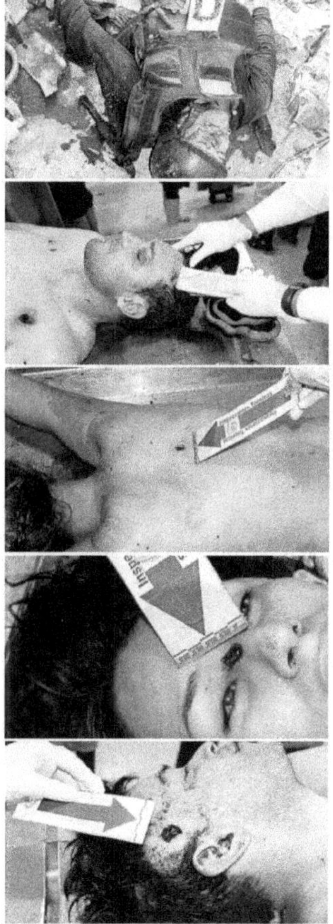

EJECUTADOS. En las dos imágenes superiores, Abraham Agostini. En la tercera y la cuarta, Lisbeth Ramírez, enfermera embarazada tiroteada en la espalda y la sien. Sobre estas líneas, probablemente Jairo Lugo. CRÓNICA / E. M.

Las investigaciones de la Fiscalía venezolana entre 2015 y 2017 ya habían determinado al menos 5.000 ejecuciones, la evidencia de que el crimen se combate a sangre y fuego y con agentes con licencia para matar y robar. Hasta ahora, la Corte Penal Internacional ha decidido mirar hacia otro lado, como bien saben los defensores de los derechos humanos de los venezolanos. El informe anual publicado por su Fiscalía ha dejado claro que Venezuela no es una prioridad frente a Filipinas y Ucrania, pese a las constantes vulneraciones. «Ha dejado entrever que no está muy satisfecha con la calidad de la información recibida», resume desde Washington el internacionalista Mariano de Alba.

«Estamos negociando, no queremos hacer frente a funcionarios, también son conocidos de nosotros. Para los que tuvieron dudas, aquí estamos, peleando. Nos han disparado, estamos agazapados. Venezuela, no pierda la esperanza, vamos a seguir por ustedes», advirtió Óscar Pérez en el primer vídeo de aquella madrugada de enero de 2018. Comenzaba así el asalto y ejecución en directo, retransmitidos a través de las redes sociales, sin censura, con la angustia a flor de piel. Alrededor del escondite en una zona montañosa, 500 militares, policías, paramilitares y agentes de las FAES, dispuestos a cobrar la pieza más cotizada para la revolución. Tres semanas antes, Maduro aprovechó uno de sus discursos televisivos para ordenar «tolerancia cero» contra «el grupo terrorista financiado por Miami». «¡Plomo con ellos, compadre!», clamó el mandatario.

Las llamadas constantes de los rebeldes a que el país acudiera en defensa «de los patriotas» no fueron atendidas. «Que el pueblo salga a la calle, es la única salida», imploró sin ningún éxito el rebelde, parapetado en el interior de la vivienda.

En el siguiente vídeo se percibe claramente las negociaciones con un mayor, situado frente a la casa, con varios de sus hombres y en actitud bastante relajada. Falsa ilusión: el drama de la muerte en directo estaba a punto de comenzar. El siguiente vídeo, donde se ve cómo los sitiados son bombardeados con lanzagranadas desde una vivienda próxima, dio la vuelta al mundo. «¡Nos disparan, nos están disparando!», clamó Pérez, con sangre en el rostro, repitiendo sus deseos de entregarse. Cientos y cientos de disparos, bombazos, el tableteo de las metralletas. «Nos quieren asesinar, nos lo acaban de decir», fueron sus últimas palabras.

El Gobierno confirmó más tarde la muerte de todo el equipo del famoso policía, pero no dejó a sus familiares acceder a la morgue, ni quiera velar a sus seres queridos. El país asistía impactado al desenlace mortal con una incógnita sin despejar: ¿quién dio la orden de acabar con sus vidas? El general Manuel Cristopher Figuera, ex director del Servicio Bolivariano de Inteligencia, aseguró en verano en la CNN que la orden de «reducirlo, eliminarlo, matarlo» procedió del presidente.

«Orden cumplida», se congratuló en televisión el *hijo de Chávez* tras conocer el desenlace del asalto a la vivienda de El Junquito. «Les digo que a cada grupo que armen y financien para traer el terrorismo le va a tocar el mismo destino», concluyó el líder bolivariano.

@danilozanomadri

Images published in the Spanish newspaper El Mundo proving that the crime against Oscar and his group was an extrajudicial execution

"

GRAND LODGES CONDEMN THE CRIMES OF MADURO AGAINST FREEMASONS

Due to the behavior that the Grand Lodge authorities had already shown, I feared that these people were hiding the chain of events that unfolded as a result of the regime's manhunt for Oscar, which included persecution, arrests, and torture of Masons.

Being the persecution of Maduro officials against members of my lodge, the main reason for my leaving the country, what I did after finding out about the state crime committed by Maduro, was to publish the details of Oscar Pérez's link on my social networks With the order, the content began to go viral.

I told the world that Oscar Pérez was a Freemason, that some of the victims who accompanied him were also, that because of him, there was persecution, arrests, and torture of Freemasons, but also alleged collaboration and cover-up of some authorities of the Grand Lodge with the Maduro regime emphasizing that they should pay attention to the conduct of the great teacher Colonel Ubaldo Jiménez Silva.

I remember that at that time, I had tremendous logistical limitations; my column in El Nacional was not active, and I was totally isolated; I knew I had to talk to someone from the top in continental Freemasonry; that's how the idea of contacting the Grand Master arose. From the Lodge of Ecuador Humberto Plaza, I had previously read him in a Twitter message; I knew that he was in open defiance against the Maduro dictatorship.

In my talk with him, I told him that Oscar Pérez and José Díaz Pimentel were members of my lodge Santiago Mariño N 208; that I met them I related how the Maduro regime had besieged our lodge, that we received police summonses, that the political police had made arrests, that there had been torture among the prisoners, I also told him that I suspected that the Past Grand Master Ubaldo Jiménez Silva had promoted the non-affiliation to Oscar Pérez, who presumed that it was his orders through the Grand Fiscal Speaker that influenced or coerced the venerable master of my lodge Rubén Rodríguez to make the Masonic trial of Oscar Pérez.

I told him that there was an alleged document circulating, supposedly signed by the Grand Master of the Grand Lodge, Colonel Jiménez Silva, and the Past Grand Secretary Alfredo Tovar, in which Oscar Pérez was declared a traitor to the country and that for this reason he should be thrown out of office. Freemasonry, I also informed him of what I knew about the criminals who assassinated Oscar Pérez, José Pimentel, and his group; I made reference to him that the mastermind was Maduro, but that Diosdado Cabello and Freddy Bernal, the latter a Freemason, were also involved expelled, that among the perpetrators was Minister of the Interior Reverol, the director of the DGCIM, Army General Iván Hernández Dala, the commander of the PNB Special Actions Force, Major Rafael Enrique Bastardo Mendoza of the Bolivarian National Guard, and the head of the operation, Lieutenant Colonel National Guard Granko Arteaga, head of the General Assistant and the Directorate of Special Affairs of the DGCIM.

I copied what Maduro had said during his speech to present the Memory and Account before the National Constituent Assembly. "This group was defeated today. I want to recognize and congratulate the PNB, the GNB, the special forces commandos of the Armed Forces, the DGCIM, and SEBIN, for dismantling this terrorist group that attacked our country. There was an armed confrontation after they were given all the guarantees to turn themselves in; 2 PNBs were riddled with shots to the head, and six seriously injured PNBs who are torn between life and death; there were more than five captured, and others were killed," Maduro said.

I told him a journalist had obtained a copy of Pérez's death certificate and posted it on Twitter. The cause of death stated in the certificate: was "Severe head trauma due to a gunshot wound to the head." Although one of his companions died from a shot that went through her neck, the others also had a coup de grace to the head.

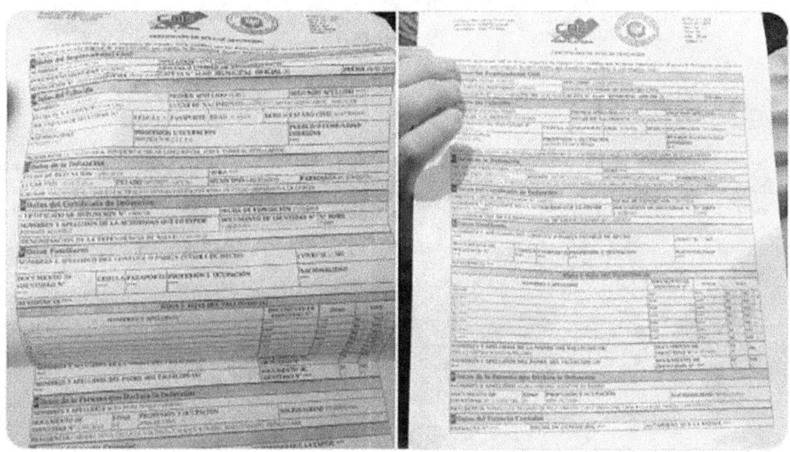

Tweet by Luz Mely: Death certificates of Oscar Pérez and Abraham Agostini, executed in the El Junquito massacre. Both were shot in the head. Neither the Prosecutor's Office nor the Defender's Office has spoken. #Venezuela

It was necessary to give this brother all the complete information, including the pros and cons, so that they, at the international level, would have a more elaborate idea of what happened in Venezuela and could address the problem. In this way, brother Humberto Plaza, Grand Master of Ecuador, became the first to issue a public condemnation against Maduro, followed by the grand lodges of Paraguay, the Dominican Republic, Brazil, Spain, Colombia, Peru, and so on. Countries until finally, the Inter-American Masonic Confederation was pronounced.

It was shocking to see how all those grand orients positioned themselves in favor of justice and defense of the truth; I tell part of this story in my article entitled "Past Grand Master of Ecuador Humberto Plaza: Venezuela is under the boot of a tyranny" published in El Nacional on September 8, 2022.

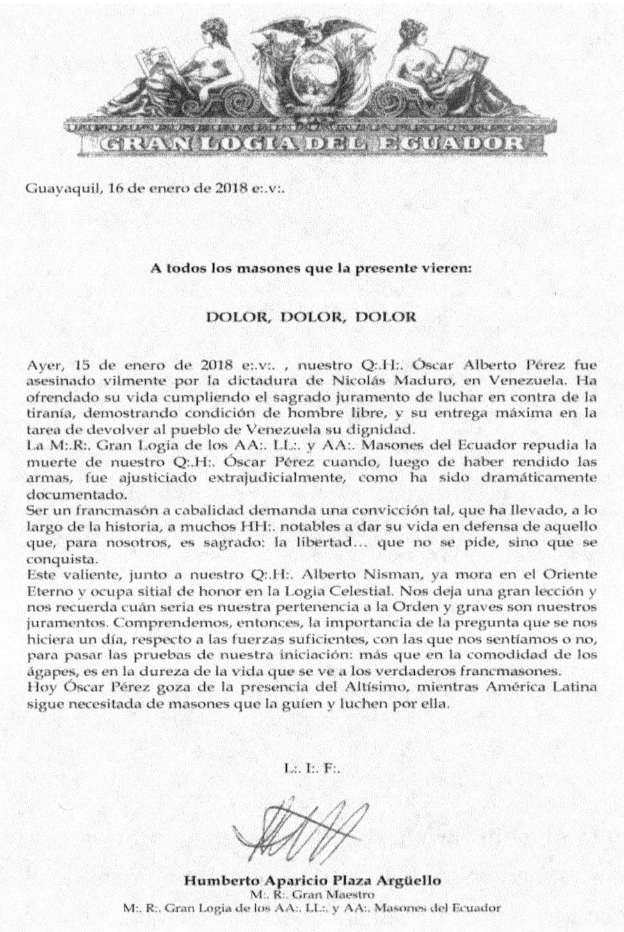

Condemnation document against Maduro issued by the Grand Lodge of Ecuador

Then the manifesto published by the Inter-American Masonic Confederation calling attention to the Grand Lodge of Venezuela for the role they played in said historical context was critical; then I share the statement, and I quote:

Transcription of the communiqué of the Inter-American Masonic Confederation on the occasion of the murder of Oscar Pérez.

The Executive Council informs all the Great Powers affiliated with the Inter-American Masonic Confederation of the following:

1) Through the international press and other broadcast channels, the extrajudicial execution of HM Oscar Alberto Pérez was made known, on the 15th of the current year, without having been subjected to due process as befits any person in a country where there is respect for human rights and dignity.

2) It has also been known that the Grand Master of the Grand Lodge of the Republic of Venezuela has issued Communiqué Number 02 of January 9, where he informs of the Masonic prosecution and the expulsion of the Order of the brother mentioned above, arguing the figures of "treason and common crimes."

3) During the commemoration of the 70th anniversary of the founding of the Inter-American Masonic Confederation in April 2017, a letter of assumption was issued, where one of the great points was the call to attention to the situation that the Republic of Venezuela is experiencing under the current dictatorial regime and urging "the members of regular Venezuelan Freemasonry to remain firm in the principles of the Masonic ideology, fighting serenely but firmly for the inexcusable respect for the national Constitution and the values of the democratic system."

4) The Executive Council of the CMI, unanimously, cannot help but regret and repudiate in the most vehement way facts like the present, where the situation reaches unacceptable extremes and where the absence of principles, values, and basic concepts of respect and human decency in those who hold some power, however brief or symbolic, lead many men and women to take desperate measures to get out of the state of anguish that their community, in general, is experiencing.

5) The concept of freedom is something many Masons and non-Masons have sacrificed their lives for. For this reason, universal Freemasonry places precious value in the highest place; for this reason, Inter-American Freemasonry has the defense of freedom, human rights,

and justice among its objectives. And for this reason, it is impossible to remain silent in the face of an aberrational situation like the one at hand.

6) What for some is categorized as treason to the Homeland for most is seen as a fight for freedom and as the only possible way to recover the rights lost due to ignorance, indifference, abuse of power, and other evils that eat away at the foundations and the very structure of those Latin American countries that still fly the flag of a perverse and failed populism.

7) To the entire Masonic community of Venezuela, we convey our deepest feeling of affection and solidarity; we ask that you do not lose faith or the nobility that you possess, that we are at your side, and we hope that this calamity that many are experiencing fronts, even outside the political sphere, soon be part of a disastrous past that no one wants to experience again and that sooner rather than later they can enjoy the right to a dignified life.

January 18, 2018

Signed: Oscar de Alfonso Ortega, President; Juan Jesús Gopar Aguilar, Vice President Zone 1; Jean-Pierre Rollet, Zone 2 Vice President; Estuardo Ordoñez Kocher, Vice President Zone 3; Jorge Díaz delgado, Vice President Zone 4; Flavio Pererira – Graff, Vice President Zone 5; Edgard Sánchez Caballero, Vice President Zone 6; Rudy Barbosa Levy, Executive Secretary.

Confederación Masónica Interamericana

Fundada el 14 de Abril de 1947

Consejo Ejecutivo

www.cmi.world

A LA COMUNIDAD MASÓNICA INTERAMERICANA

El Consejo Ejecutivo hace conocer a todas las Grandes Potencias afiliadas a la Confederación Masónica Interamericana lo siguiente:

1) Por medio de la prensa internacional y otros canales de difusión se ha tomado conocimiento de la ejecución extrajudicial del HM Oscar Alberto Pérez, de Venezuela, en fecha 15 de los corrientes, sin haber sido sometido a un debido proceso como corresponde a cualquier persona en un país donde existe respeto por los derechos y la dignidad humana.

2) También se ha conocido que el Gran Maestro de la Gran Logia de la República de Venezuela ha emitido el Comunicado No. 02, del 9 de enero pasado, donde hace saber del enjuiciamiento masónico y la expulsión de la Orden del referido Hermano, argumentando las figuras jurídicas de "traición a la Patria y delitos comunes".

3) Durante la conmemoración de los 70 años de fundación de la Confederación Masónica Interamericana, en abril de 2017, se emitió la Carta de Asunción, donde uno de los puntos sobresalientes fue el llamado de atención a la situación que vive la República de Venezuela bajo el actual régimen dictatorial e instando *"a los miembros de la Masonería venezolana regular a mantenerse firmes en los principios del ideario masónico, bregando serena pero firmemente por el respeto inexcusable a la Constitución Nacional y a los valores del sistema democrático."*

4) El Consejo Ejecutivo de la CMI, de manera unánime, no puede menos que lamentar y repudiar de la manera mas vehemente hechos como el presente, donde la situación llega a extremos inadmisibles y donde la ausencia de principios, valores y conceptos básicos de respeto y decencia humana en quienes detentan algún tipo de poder, por muy efímero o simbólico que sea, llevan a muchos hombres y mujeres a tomar medidas desesperadas con tal de salir del estado de angustia que vive su comunidad en general.

5) El concepto de libertad es algo por lo cual muchos masones y no masones han sacrificado su vida. Por eso, la Masonería universal coloca ese preciado valor en el sitial mas elevado; por eso, la Masonería Interamericana tiene entre sus objetivos la defensa de la libertad, los derechos humanos y la justicia. Y por eso también, no es posible callar ante una situación aberrante como la que nos ocupa.

6) Lo que para algunos es categorizado como traición a la Patria para los mas es visto como una lucha por la libertad y como la única forma posible para recuperar los derechos perdidos por causa de la ignorancia, la indiferencia, el abuso de poder y otros males que carcomen los cimientos y la propia estructura de aquellos países latinoamericanos que aun enarbolan la bandera de un populismo perverso y fallido.

7) A toda la comunidad masónica de Venezuela les hacemos llegar nuestro mas profundo sentimiento de afecto y solidaridad, les pedimos que no pierdan ni la fe ni la nobleza que poseen, que estamos a su lado y esperamos que esa calamidad que están viviendo en muchos frentes, incluso fuera del ámbito político, pronto sea parte de un pasado nefasto que nadie quiere volver a experimentar y que mas pronto que tarde puedan disfrutar del derecho a una vida digna.

18 de enero de 2018

Firmado: Oscar de Alfonso Ortega, Presidente; Juan Jesús Gopar Aguilar, Vicepresidente Zona 1; Jean-Pierre Rollet, Vicepresidente Zona 2; Estuardo Ordoñez Kocher, Vicepresidente Zona 3; Jorge Diaz Delgado, Vicepresidente Zona 4; Flávio Pereira-Graff, Vicepresidente Zona 5; Edgar Sánchez Caballero, Vicepresidente Zona 6; Rudy Barbosa Levy, Secretario Ejecutivo.

Image capture copy of the IMC pronouncement document condemning the Maduro regime

After the pronouncement of the CMI, more than 30 lodges from all over the world followed, condemning the Maduro regime for the death of the brothers Oscar Pérez and José Pimentel. All this happened because I dared to send the information directly to the international powers. I think that he would never have found out due to the alleged cover-up of the directive of the Grand Lodge under the grand mastery of Colonel Jiménez Silva.

COMPLAINT FORCED DISAPPEARANCE OF FREEMASONS

Esteban Oria entevista a Endry Mendez

The persecution of Freemasons had not ended with the arrests of Freemasons in my lodge between January and March 2018. Then in 2021, I discovered two other crimes against Freemasons connected to the Oscar Pérez case in 2018.

I had been taken by surprise by the contact that brother Endry Méndez made with me; it was the year 2021, and he told me that he had just arrived in Paraguay seeking political refuge; it was he who told me that Maduro's hunt for Masons had not ended with the death of Oscar Pérez, told me that he investigated the disappearance of two other Freemasons, probably linked to the alleged order to eliminate an alleged support network of Oscar Pérez Freemasons.

What is known is that even after the brothers Oscar Pérez and Pimentel were assassinated, the Maduro regime continued to repress and search for freemasons allied to Oscar. The national and international press exposed these facts.

Press release denouncing trespassing in lodges

The disappearances allegedly occurred in mid-2018, just after the deaths of the freemasons Oscar Pérez and José Pimentel; they were state officials, the first of which is William Muñoz, who served as commissioner of the SEBIN Bolivarian Intelligence Service; his disappearance was reported on July 15, 2018. Then the disappearance of Colonel Juan Hurtado, in charge of the weapons park of the Presidential Honor Guard, was reported missing in September 2018, according to the UN A/HRC report. /44/54 from June 15 to July 3, 2020.

Commissioner Wilmer Muñoz denounced as a missing member of SEBIN.

Detective Méndez tells me that he was able to obtain the last location of Commissioner Muñoz through call tracking in the windward region known as El Guapo. While investigating the case, he resorted to various sources to gather data; in the same way, he requested support from his investigation unit at the CICPC. However, he obtained refusals that led him to confront the directive of the police force headed by the figure of its director Douglas Rico, director of the Criminal and Forensic Scientific Investigation Corps.

Endry Méndez next to brother Oscar Pérez's helicopter

The detective suspects Commissioner Muñoz may have been in Oscar Pérez's telephone contacts. Detective Endry has a theory that this official was subjected to some retaliation or promoted on some alleged elimination list by officials of the regime. He tells me his body was probably thrown into a river with piranhas.

The investigation that Detective Endry carried out on Lieutenant Colonel Juan Hurtado also lacked support from the competent bodies, but he even raised suspicions against him at the DGCIM office in the Miraflores palace.

Colonel Juan Hurtado, denounced by international organizations as forced disappearance

I can vouch for what Endry says since I spoke with relatives of both victims. Regarding Hurtado, I learned from that source that the lieutenant colonel was allegedly linked to a suspicious disappearance of armament in his custody, which they later found. The source confirmed that an ONG had filed a report of his disappearance with the competent bodies in matters of human rights in the United States. It explains why his disappearance is reviewed by the United Nations human rights office, appearing in the Bachelet report of November 21, 2021.

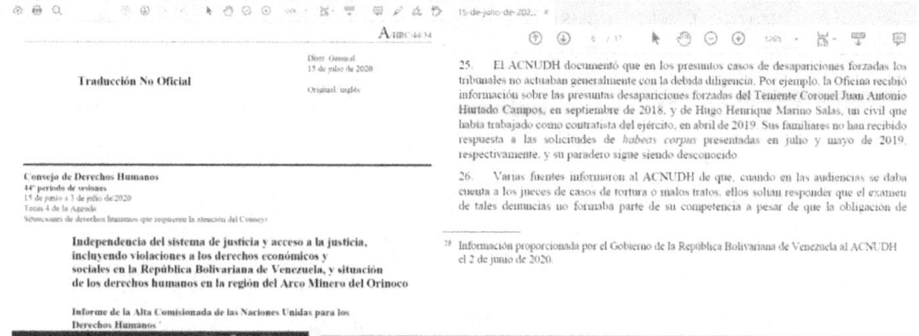

Report of the UN human rights council reports Juan Hurtado as a forced disappearance.

The detective comments that he received a call from a high-ranking member of the military to warn him that, as a result of his investigation, he was being monitored by military counterintelligence and therefore recommended that he stop investigating him.

Masonic Passport of Endry Mendez

Regarding the cause of the disappearance of Lieutenant Colonel Hurtado, Detective Endry Méndez reached the same conclusion that both Masons were on Oscar's contact list and could have been mistaken as conspirators, the detective's conclusion is that they were probably promoted in those lists of enforced disappearances from Maduro's counterintelligence agencies that are so often mentioned in human rights reports.

Detective Endry told me that he came to these investigations due to a request made to him by the Grand Lodge in the figure of Alfredo Tovar and Ubaldo Jiménez; it was in this way that he was able to meet with the wives of these officials and corroborate those stories to start both investigations.

Due to his high level of exposure when he did his job, he received threats to his life, which is how he requested protection from the authorities of the aforementioned Grand Lodge (Alfredo and Ubaldo); the response he received was the abandonment of his fate.

The investigation cost him to exile in Paraguay, a country he received and installed socially. During his stay, an unfortunate event happened while driving a taxi in an alleged robbery of his vehicle; he was seriously injured, and the bullet grazed his heart. Endry thinks it was an attempt on his life carried out by Maduro agents; the case is still open with the Paraguayan police.

Endry has been cared for by Paraguayan medicine and supported by the Freemasons fraternity, who have helped him recover. However, he is still convalescing due to the seriousness of his injury and is waiting for help that will allow him to travel to France to seek rehabilitation and recover.

The testimony of Endry Méndez has reached the International Criminal Court. It is part of the compendium that is helping the international justice system to clarify the facts of human rights violations in Venezuela.

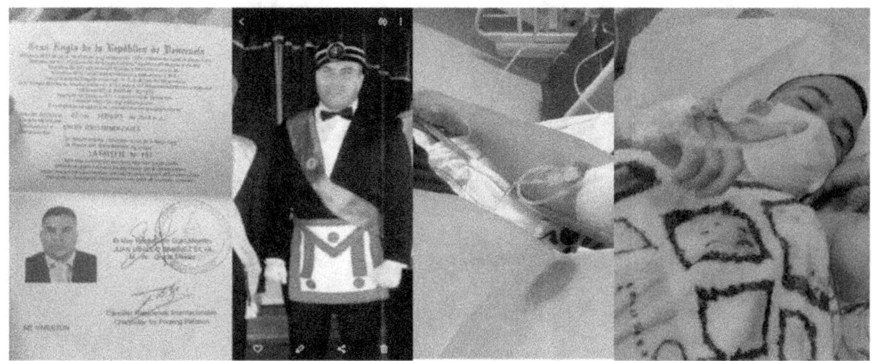

Endry Méndez, exiled in Paraguay, suffered an attack and was seriously injured; he was treated by Paraguayan doctors and is recovering.

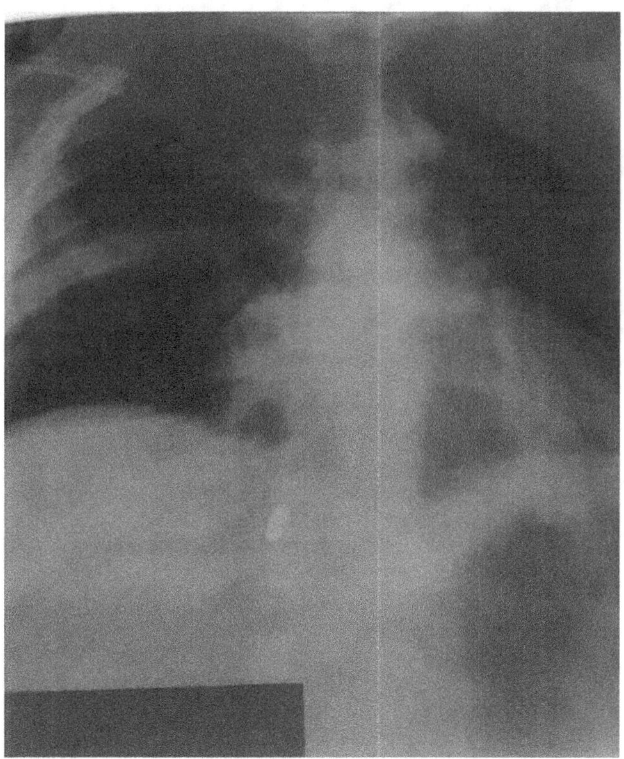

Radio X shows the bullet that Detective Endry Méndez received

About the disappearance of Colonel Juan Hurtado, in a show of cynicism, the Minister of Defense, Vladimir Padrino López, published a poster from the ministry declaring Lieutenant Colonel Juan Hurtado, a deserter for not showing up for his duties in the command. It is a criminal regime like Maduro's, which mocks intelligence.

Maduro's political police are also skilled in changing the testimonies of witnesses; these officials reach the victims' relatives to coerce them to make them change their versions or force them to stop looking for their relatives; it often happens with the defenseless families living within Venezuelan territory.

Detective Endry Méndez maintains that the director of the CICPC, General Commissioner Douglas Rico, has knowledge of the identity of the military counterintelligence officials and SEBIN who disappeared both Commissioner Wilmer Muñoz and Colonel Juan Hurtado; he thinks that international organizations should call him to appear and testify.

Detective Endry Méndez appointed Commissioner Douglas Rico to protect the identity of the officials who perpetrated the disappearance of Commissioner Wilmer Muñoz.

I have published an article dedicated to Detective Endry's complaint titled "Ex-investigator of the Grand Lodge denounces Maduro for the disappearance of Masons," published in El Nacional dated July 28, 202.

WILLIAM JIMENEZ WITNESS BEFORE THE ICC AND POLITICAL ASYLEE IN THE NETHERLANDS

William Jimenez interviewed by Esteban Oria

Once I exposed the persecution of Freemasons by the Maduro dictatorship in 2019, the Freemason and friend William Jiménez, visiting member of the Santiago Mariño Lodge Number 208, with whom I have been friends for more than 20 years, contacted me. Even though he worked as a state official, Jiménez has always been a consistent regime opponent, focused on denouncing and fighting for democracy.

When he called me, he told me that he was in Venezuela but that he would soon leave the country because he feared for his life; because he knew of irregularities committed by Maduro officials related to the Oscar Pérez case, he asked me to help him spread them. in the press once you are in the safe zone.

William's position was that of former coordinator of Strategic Investigations of Senamecf and the Bello Monte morgue; he is also a lawyer and Human Rights representative at the Caracas Bar Association.

When William arrived in Peru, he obtained an exclusive interview with the journalist Sebastiana Barráez; in that interview, he denounced Diosdado Cabello for ordering the cremation of the body of former Cicpc Oscar Pérez to disappear evidence of extrajudicial executions. William witnessed an intense discussion between the people of Diosdado Cabello and the team of Padrino López, defense minister because the latter opposed the cremation.

William Jiménez posing at the entrance of the Grand Lodge of Venezuela

William shared with me the statement that he gave to Sebastiana Barráez replicated in various news portals to copy it in this book. He said at that time that "there was so much concern among government and police officials about what could happen with the death of the pilot Oscar Pérez, that some thought about leaving the country. When it was believed that the corpse would be cremated and with it, there would be a violent reaction from his followers; some prepared themselves. That night, Commissioner José Humberto Ramírez Márquez, current director of Senamecf, had already left for San Antonio del Táchira, about to cross the border," revealed the former official.

"He details that on Friday, January 19, there were already orders from the Second Court of Military Control to inhume -bury- the bodies. The letters arrived at Senamecf on Friday around 6 in the afternoon. Family members were notified on Saturday. And that day, the bodies left for Táchira and Maracaibo. But nobody knew what would be done with the body of Oscar Pérez." Lugo." In this part of the statement, William points to General Bladimir Lugo, whom I denounced when I was a colonel in charge of security for the federal palace, for letting the colectivos in during the assault on parliament in 2017. "But on Saturday, January 20, and after, as he added, due to certain "political" movements, Óscar Pérez's father appeared to try to remove the body - although he had never recognized it - Colonel (GNB) Bladimir burst onto the scene.

William continues with his story: "He arrived with the order to cremate the body of Oscar Pérez and showed up with four military units full of guards and tripled security (...) Colonel Lugo told Colonel García - director of Senamecf - what following: 'Look, Colonel, I have ordered much higher than Reverol's, and be careful that you are absent because the orders I have been to put you and anyone else who goes crazy in jail (...) Colonel Lugo's orders were to take the body of Oscar Pérez at half past one in the morning, take it out to the crematorium, and turn it into dust. They ordered us to send for the head of the crematorium, Ángeles Colmenares", narrates Jiménez Gavidia.

The journalist explicitly asks the interviewee the following:

"Did Colonel Lugo tell Colonel García that he had orders to take Oscar Pérez's body to be cremated?" To which the former official replied: "Yes, he told him. And also that the order was from Diosdado Cabello."

He also continues with his story: "In fact, that night, the greatest pressure General Reverol received was from Diosdado Cabello because Reverol did not want to cremate the body, but Diosdado did. Even so, Reverol called Colonel García to tell him to cremate the body. The colonel replied: "Understood, Major General, but the Law prevents me from doing so."

That same night there was a meeting at the Court Martial in which, according to the source, Major (Ex) Luis Marval, military prosecutor Ninth National Senior Military Prosecutor, Lieutenant Colonel Elías Plasencia, and the second military judge of Control, Tcnel, were present. There they would have discussed the actions to be taken with Pérez's body: Jose Rafael Mejia Lopez.

"Colonel García said that the Senamecf Law does not authorize him to anything other than burial." William says that he told them that "if those present ordered the body of Oscar Pérez to be cremated, they would be committing the Venezuelan State to violations of Human Rights and being the subject of actions before the International Court of Justice in The Hague."

Another meeting of the Military High Command would have been held with Minister Vladimir Padrino López at the head, who supposedly was the ones who made the final decision:

"We went to the Senamecf, and before midnight, General Edgar José Rojas Borges, president of the Martial Court, calls the colonel and notifies him: 'The citizen President of the Republic welcomes the decision made by the Military High Command which orders compliance through the office of the Minister of Defense, GJ Vladimir Padrino López, for which he is instructed to carry out the controlled burial, taking the appropriate security measures.' Shortly after, he called MG Reverol and ratified the decision, indicating that the body of Oscar Pérez should be in the cemetery at 6 in the morning on January 21," added Gaviria.

Another irregularity denounced by Jiménez, a Freemason visiting member of the Santiago Mariño Lodge Number 208, is that the death certificates were signed by doctors who never saw the corpses. Jiménez told me that the orders were given to alter the toxicological tests on the bodies to make public opinion see that Oscar Pérez and his group were drugged. "Reverol told the colonel: I need to have those tests now and that they are reflected in them that they (Oscar Pérez and his group) had consumed alcohol or drugs."

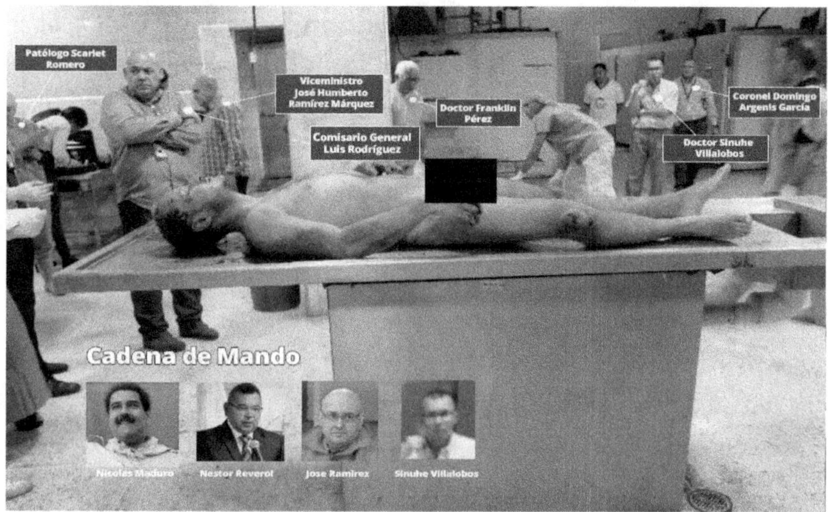

Chain of Command during the autopsy of Oscar Pérez

William Jiménez was the first to denounce that what happened to Oscar Pérez was an extrajudicial execution; he said that he could tell when he observed the bullet impacts on the body and the orientation that the trajectory of the bullets could have had; how close the perpetrators could be. He wrote a report on the irregularities in his knowledge. He handed them over to the prosecutor Luisa Ortega Díaz who raised him as a witness before the International Criminal Court.

In my opinion column in El Nacional, I have written an article entitled "William Jiménez identifies suspects in the former prosecutor's report delivered to the ICC." This very important post makes a significant contribution to the investigation carried out by the Criminal Court prosecutor. International Karim Khan, because it exposes and identifies with names and surnames a part of the chain of command that was present at the Junquito massacre, as the act in which Oscar Pérez was executed is known, it is about the group of officials present during the autopsy of the executed bodies.

With the permission of William Jiménez, we published one of the photos from the prosecutor's report where Oscar Pérez's body can be seen on the surgical table of the autopsy room surrounded by these officials that William Jiménez was able to identify.

William begins by identifying Commissioner General Luis Rodríguez, whom he recognizes by his khaki shirt and posing with crossed arms, he was the deputy director of the national forensic service; Behind him was Commissioner General José Humberto Ramírez Márquez, Vice Minister of the Integrated Criminal Investigation System, attached to the Ministry of People's Power for Internal Relations, Justice and Peace, which in his time was directed by Major General Néstor Luis Reverol Torres, of the On the left side you can see the pathologist Scarlet Romero making notes on the person who performed the autopsy on Abraham Noé Lugo Ramos and on Daniel Enrique Soto Torres; in the center is Dr. Franklin Pérez, he was the one who performed the autopsy on Abraham Agostini and Abraham Lugo Ramos, and the female Lisbeth Andreína Ramírez; We are seeing Dr. Sinuhe Villalobos, head of legal medical examination at the national level, the area that directs forensic doctors, with a yellow shirt and crossed hands; he is the man who was present at the scene of the crime in El Junquito, where the removal of the corpse corresponds according to the law, according to William, what is striking is that although he carried out these removals, he did not subscribe to them; on the contrary, he made subordinate doctors sign acts that they did not even witness, he will have a lot to explain before the competent justice agencies. Behind the doctor, in a lilac shirt and blue pants, is Colonel Domingo Argenis García Pérez, director of the national service of medicine and forensic service, reporting to Minister Reverol.

In addition, William shared with me the report of the prosecutor Luisa Ortega Díaz, the same document given to the prosecutor Karim Khan of the International Criminal Court. The compendium includes more than

300 images, with expert explanations of both the crime scene and each of the murdered victims. I read each page carefully; it allowed me to understand and learn about the criminal elements and the circumstances involved in that crime.

The report corroborates the extrajudicial execution against the freemasons Oscar Pérez, José Díaz Pimentel, and the rest of the group that accompanied them. The report confirms that Oscar's group surrendered, did not return enemy fire, turned themselves into Maduro's agents, and was assassinated with shots to the head.

JOSÉ ESTEBAN ORIA

Víctima: OSCAR ALBERTO PÉREZ C.I 15.948.499

Precinto con numeración de autopsia: **NO VISIBLE EN LAS FOTOGRAFÍAS INSERTAS**
Marcaje asignado durante las fijaciones fotográficas del sitio de suceso: **(2A) PARTE INTERNA DE LA VIVIENDA**

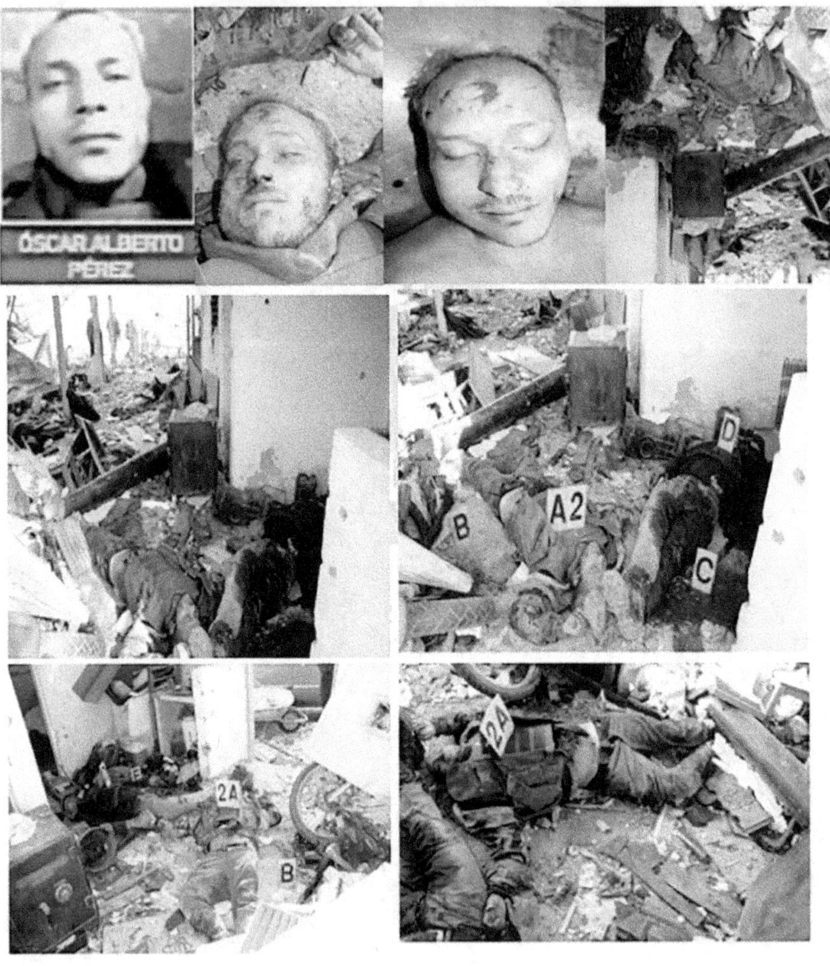

Print Copy CPI report details of the body of brother Oscar Pérez

EXPOSICIÓN FOTOGRÁFICA EN FORMATO DIGITAL N° 05

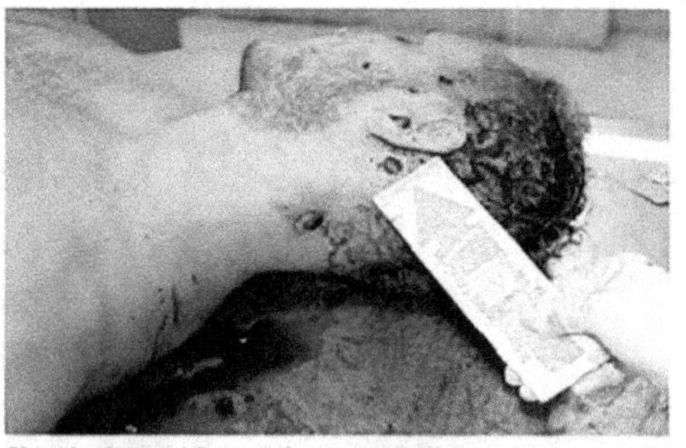 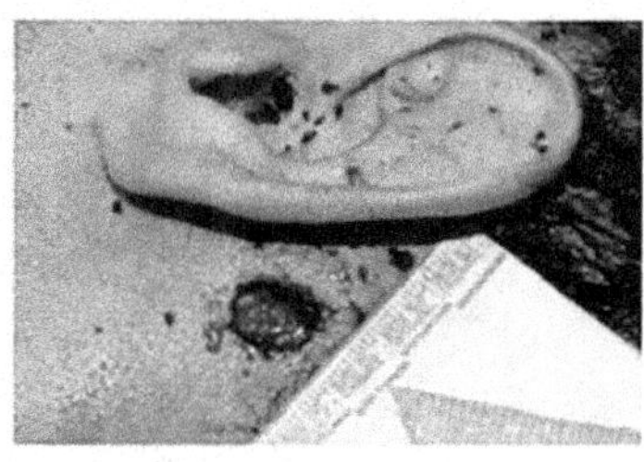

En la presente fijación fotográfica en formato digital se observa, en carácter general y de detalle, señalado con testigo flecha y métrico, herida abierta penetrante de forma circular, al proyectar el testigo métrico se determina un diámetro aproximado de 12mm, el cual tiene bordes regulares con paredes tapizadas con restos negruzcos mezclados con sangre, localizado en región retroauricular izquierda; abundantes costras hemáticas desecadas y otorragia izquierda, dicha lesión tiene características macroscópicas compatibles con orificio de entrada, lo cual debió ser corroborado en la autopsia con la trayectoria intraorganica y estudio histopatológico del tejido periorificial.

EXPOSICIÓN FOTOGRÁFICA EN FORMATO DIGITAL N° 06

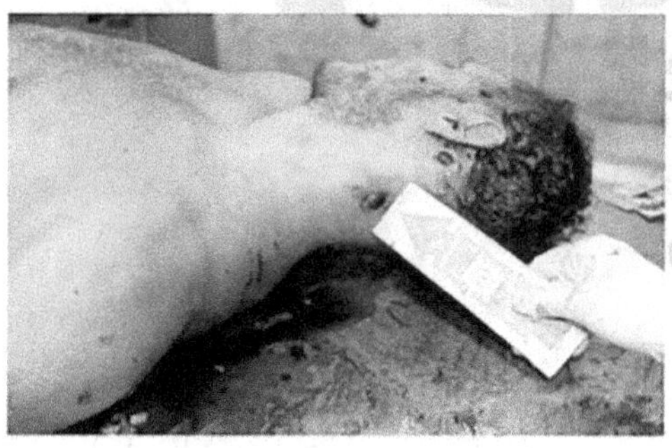 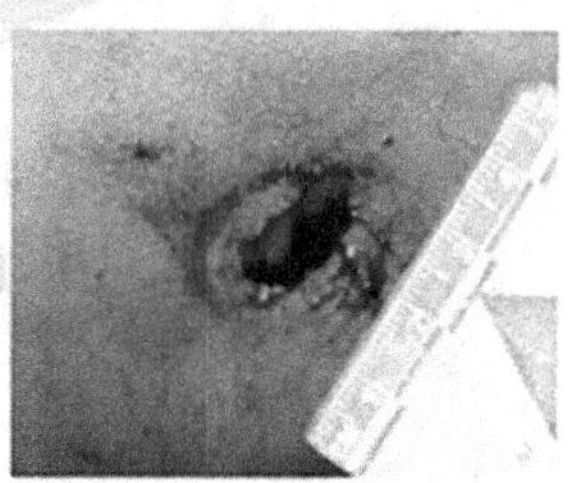

En la presente fijación fotográfica en formato digital se observa, en carácter general y de detalle, señalado con testigo flecha y métrico, orificio de entrada de contacto, con signo de Puppe Werkgartne, al proyectar el testigo métrico mide 20 x 10mm, el cual tiene bordes irregulares con anillo contuso, localizado en región latero-cervical izquierda, dicho orificio debió ser corroborado en la autopsia con la trayectoria intraorganica y estudio histopatológico del tejido periorificial.

Evidence of execution on the body of Oscar Pérez

The photos in the report show the state of his body; it was a shock to see these images; those of brother José Díaz Pimentel cannot be shown; they practically removed half of his skull and part of his face.

William's testimony has been able to identify this group of officials; we hope ,they will be called to testify before the International Criminal Court in due course.

KNOW WHO ARE THE RESPONSIBLES FOR CRIMES AGAINST HUMANITY ACCORDING TO THE HUMAN RIGHTS ORGANIZATIONS

Responsible for crimes against humanity according to the UN, chain of command indicated in the UN report, from left to right, Nicolas Maduro, Delcy Rodríguez, Diosdado Cabello, Tarek Al Aisami, Bottom left to right, Asdrúbal José Brito Hernández, Iván Hernández Dala, Gustavo Enrique González López, Alexander Granko Arteaga.

The identity of the material authors of the crimes of the freemasons Oscar Pérez and José Pimentel, and the group that accompanied them, but also of crimes, is known through the work of the press. A recent report published by the United Nations International Mission has specifically stated that the participation of the Venezuelan State in the repression of dissent has been demonstrated, that they have committed crimes, including acts of torture and sexual violence, and highlighted the role of the two military and civilian intelligence services of Venezuela, "which would be a fundamental part of the human rights violations: the General Directorate of Military Counterintelligence (DGCIM) and the Bolivarian National Intelligence Service (SEBIN)." In addition, it is pointed out that such crimes are part of the "execution of a plan orchestrated by President

Maduro and other high-level authorities to repress the opposition to the Government."

Many of those named in the UN report are the same ones who have been reported as allegedly responsible for the masterminds in this crime against the freemasons Oscar Pérez and José Pimentel and the group that accompanied them, beginning with the masterminds Nicolas Maduro and Diosdado Cabello. And as material authors, Alexander Granko Arteaga, Douglas Rico, and Minister Néstor Reverol are indicated.

Due to his complaints, William Jiménez, another of the Freemasons who had to go into exile to save his life, filed his request for political asylum with the authorities of the Kingdom of Holland. Among the arguments presented is his position as a state official who denounced allegedly illegal actions, violation of the human rights of his superiors about the Oscar Pérez case, also his status as a Freemason, visiting member of the lodge where Oscar Pérez was affiliated, William is member of the Adhoc group International Masonic Commission on Human Rights, created by the Venezuelan Federation of Political Scientists, whose members are complainant Masons who have sent letters to the office of the International Criminal Court about the disappearances of the Masons William Muñoz and Juan Hurtado. All these arguments presented are of sufficient weight to consider his life threatened and therefore deserving of state protection.

To tell you briefly what happened with his asylum case, the immigration officer denied him, placing him in a deportation situation; William had to appeal the decision in court; despite not having money, he found support from a group of lawyers who defended him before the court, they shared with the Judge press material with the denunciations made by William, they also include the journalistic reviews of the persecution suffered by the Freemasons, the denunciations of the Adhoc group of the Commission, all this allowed to demonstrate that William Jiménez's life was in danger, the Dutch court has decided to protect him with refugee status.

William told me that he remembers the moment when he accompanied Oscar Pérez's coffin to his final resting place in the cemetery; the press described him dressed in a black tie and white shirt; he told the press that the reason for his presence dressed in that way was to pay respect to his brother, a mason dressed in order, as they tell the masons. He was the only Freemason present during the funeral ceremony. Today William Jiménez patiently awaits his turn to be called to make a statement before the International Criminal Court as a witness.

In this exclusive interview with Primer Informe, William Jiménez, former Head of the Bello Monte Morgue, who revealed for the first time the images of the execution of former police agent Oscar Pérez, denounces how the Nicolás Maduro regime uses morgues

The life of William Jimenez is in danger, an eyewitness in the crime against Oscar Perez

ANGEL FAJARDO, FIRST POLITICAL ASYLUM FOR HIS CONDITION AS A MASON PERSECUTED IN VENEZUELA

Esteban Oria talking with Angel Fajardo for his opinion column for El Nacional

I recently had the opportunity to talk with Ángel Fajardo, a member of the Santiago Marino N 208 lodge, a good friend with whom I shared in my lodge; I am glad to know that he had received political asylum in France.

Ángel told me about the odyssey he went through to obtain the protection of the French State. He could not go to the Venezuelan Freemasonry to corroborate his story since he knew that the authorities of the Grand Lodge under the leadership of Colonel Ubaldo Jimenez Silva were committed to the Maduro regime.

During the asylum application process, Angel could not appeal to any document issued by the Grand Lodge in his favor; the truth is that there is no official documentation from the Grand Lodge denouncing the human rights violations that were committed against the Freemasons during

Maduro's hunt for the Freemason Oscar Pérez that resulted in the death of all Oscar's companions through extrajudicial executions.

So the asylum case of the Freemason brother Ángel Fajardo lacked witnesses, so he was denied in the first instance at the migration office. The immigration officer did not believe the danger his life was running for, having been part of the same lodge Oscar Pérez attended.

Then it happened that brother Ángel Fajardo appealed the decision before the Human Rights Court, looking for a new lawyer,. They began investigating the facts, finding enough press material to confirm Ángel's testimony.

Ángel's legal defense shared with the Judge these press reports denouncing the persecution of Freemasons by DGCIM agents, as well as the communiqués from the Grand Lodges condemning the state crime committed by Maduro against the freemasons Oscar Pérez and José Pimentel. The Judge was impressed with the atrocities committed by Maduro against the Freemasons; for the role of his government's repression of Venezuelans. Thus, the Judge's verdict ruled in favor of political asylum for Angel and his wife, becoming the first Venezuelan Freemason in the history of Venezuela to receive political asylum for political persecution against Freemasons.

What the Judge's minutes say is that the applicants "ask the court to annul the decision of June 19, 2018, by which the director general of the French Office for the Protection of Refugees and Stateless Persons (OFPRA) rejected their request for asylum and recognize her as a refugee or, failing that, grant her the benefit of subsidiary protection".

This request for subsidiary protection was not a political asylum; brother Ángel only asked France to recognize his vulnerability and at least extend the period, but the Judge went much further.

I am going to share with you what the Judge wrote of his statement; the idea of this paragraph is to make a big exclamation that serves to visualize the seriousness of danger in which we, the opposition Masons of the lodge Santiago Mariño Number 208, who led to a French court to recognize the endangered state of a Venezuelan citizen due to his status as a dissident Freemason due to systematic persecution carried out by Maduro against Freemasons opposed to his regime. Below I transcribe extracts from the document.

(...) Mr. FAJARDO GONZALEZ was a member of Freemasonry. Since April 2017, he has attended the Santiago Lodge. Marino, whom he officially joined on September 2, in which he met Óscar Pérez, an opponent of the Nicolás Maduro regime. Upon learning that the latter had fled, he told one of his lodge members that he could help the fugitive reach the Colombian border. His proposal, however, went unanswered. He also wrote an article about liberty, equality, fraternity, and democracy he broadcast in his lodge.

On December 6, 2017, he and his wife left their country to visit his daughter. In France, they learned that on January 15, 2018, Oscar Pérez had been assassinated by the Venezuelan authorities, who are currently looking for accomplices or sympathizers of the latter, considered a terrorist. They also learned that Freemasonry was subject to reprisals for having exposed this murder, they cannot return without fear to their country, which is mired in insecurity, and one of his sons has just fled.

The decision of the French Court that grants political asylum to Ángel Fajardo for the Oscar Pére case
4. From his statements, it appears that he is a member of Freemasonry; the applicant joined the Santiago Marino lodge in 2017, whose opponent to the regime Óscar Pérez was a member. He was also able to evoke the context in which he finds himself. Several times in the lodge, he met the latter whose ideas he shared. He also evoked in spontaneous terms his opposition to the Nicolás Maduro regime. In addition, available public sources, including press articles, expose that the Masonic lodges in Latin America have condemned the death of Óscar Pérez, and the Nicolas Maduro regime has retaliated against people related to the latter (Oscar Pérez), including masons. Articles from the Venezuelan newspaper TalCual and the El Pitazo website, dated January 2018, point to an

investigation carried out by the General Directorate of Military Counterintelligence of Venezuela against potential allies of Óscar Pérez within the Masonic lodges. Thus, it follows from what precedes that, in the particular circumstances of the case, Mr. Fajardo González was rightly feared in the sense of the provisions mentioned above of the Geneva Convention.

The general principles of law applicable to refugees, resulting in particular from the provisions of the Geneva Convention, impose, to fully guarantee the refugee the protection provided by the convention above, that the same status be recognized for the person of the same nationality. Who was married to a refugee on the date the latter applied for refugee status or had a sufficiently stable and continuous relationship with him to form a family with him,

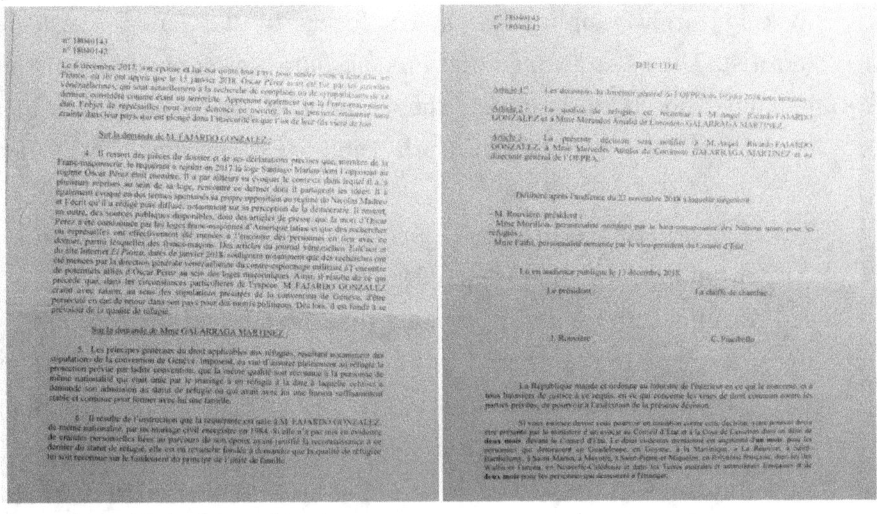

Print copy of Angel Fajardo's asylum document

HE DECIDED:

Article 15: — The decisions of the General Director of OFPRA of June 19, 2018, are annulled

Article 2: Refugee status is recognized for Mr. Ángel Ricardo FAJARDO GONZALEZ and Mrs. XXXXXXXX XXXXXX.

Article 3: This decision will be notified to Mr. Angel Ricardo FAJARDO GONZALEZ, to Mrs. XXXXXXXXXXXX, and to the General Director of OFPRA.

Deliberated after the hearing on November 22, 2018, in which the following met:

– Mr Rouvière, President; . .

– Ms. Morillon, designee of the United Nations High Commissioner for

refugees; to

– Ms. Fathi, appointed by the Vice President of the Council of State. End of quote.

The French state currently protects Brother Ángel Fajardo due to the persecution of Freemasons by Maduro officials in the Oscar Pérez case.

I am pleased to know that the work we have been doing to publicize Maduro's hunt against the Freemasons in the press is paying off. The publications in the media and the documents issued by the grand lodges have been fundamental in defending asylums for the Freemasons directly affected by this hunt for Maduro. It is my wish that all those involved are protected. It is their right that in the case of Ángel Fajardo, the criterion of an indirect victim of human rights violation applies to a great extent.

State agent: the individual who loses his life, who suffers in his integrity or freedom, which is deprived of his patrimony, in violation of the conventional precepts in which these rights are collected. To learn a little more in-depth about the concept of indirect victim and how it applies, according to the tradition in legislation, the concept of direct victim refers to the person against whom the illicit conduct of the victim is directed immediately, explicitly, and deliberately. On the other hand, the concept of indirect victim refers to a subject who does not suffer the illegal conduct in the same way as the direct victim but also finds his rights affected by the impact received by the so-called direct victim, in such a way that The damage that she suffers is produced as an effect of the one that she has suffered, but once the violation reaches her, she becomes an injured person under her title. Thus, it can be said that the damage suffered by an indirect victim is an "effect or consequence" of the affectation experienced by the direct victim. In this vein, the paradigmatic example of indirect victims is the relatives of people who have directly and immediately suffered a violation of their human rights, which in the case of Freemasons, refers to all those members of the lodge Santiago Mariño Number 208 in which Oscar Pérez was affiliated, specifically those summoned, arrested, tortured. Those who escaped due to credible fear and went into exile also apply to the Grand Lodge members who have investigated the cases of Masons forcibly disappearing due to their relationship with Oscar Pérez.

FROM EXILE COMMITTED TO FREEDOM

After what happened to Oscar Pérez and José Pimentel and the arrests made of the other Masons of my lodge, I knew that it would be hazardous to return to Venezuela. So I decided to stay in the United States and apply for political asylum. I admit that I fear for my life and that of my family; Maduro is a criminal who has no qualms about harming and doing harm; I chose to take the most sensible option at the cost of losing everything in my country.

This decision irreversibly affected my life, to the point that I could not be with my parents in their final days; that was the most significant pain he felt; it is indescribable to see how your loved ones die and not being able to do anything beyond limited financial assistance.

In Venezuela, medicine is a dead letter; it does not have a functional health system or medicines; it was tough for me to see the light of my parent's life go out in a state of absolute precariousness. I can summarize that moment of my life as the most terrible period ever experienced; the fact of not even have been able to hug and accompany them in those final hours is perhaps the most significant trauma and pain that I carry with me; it is the reason why I am like the ant, working without fainting until I see my country free of Maduro and his people; until freedom returns to our lives, that's what the teaching my parents sowed took advantage of; to love freedom.

The truth is that the events in my lodge were primarily responsible for my departure from Venezuela. Despite having suffered the sieges and assaults on our Federation offices at the El Nacional de El Silencio headquarters, also in my work in the National Assembly, that was what happened with Maduro's persecution of the Masons of my lodge with the object to hunt down Oscar Pérez, the trigger for my departure from Venezuela.

How Maduro acted with the arrests and torture after the deaths of Oscar, Pimentel, and their group led me to denounce those deaths before instances such as the Grand Orients exposed me to the regime, I also had to denounce the alleged collaboration of the Grand Master of my Grand Lodge, Colonel Ubaldo Jiménez Silva with the Maduro regime, he is probably not alone in this.

There are the irrefutable facts, freemasons victims of crimes considered against humanity; we have people who were arrested, tortured, and missing freemasons; we have people in exile persecuted, there are injuries, some of them live in vulnerable areas and exposed to the hunt for Maduro.

Perhaps it can cause me an inevitable discouragement when I find out that some victims do not denounce their perpetrators or executioners or allow themselves to be intimidated and remain silent, also people who cover up the repressors out of fear, the truth is that the consequence of cohabiting with the regime of Maduro, by not denouncing the crimes that are committed knowingly, is the servitude and maintenance of the reign of terror of Nicolas Maduro and his military entourage.

I have maintained my positions for many years, warning about the dangerousness of the Maduro regime through my opinion column in El Nacional and other media. I consider the Maduro regime the worst threat to democracies on the continent. They use the immense oil fortune under our territory to finance parties and political figures from all countries and influence politicians in their decisions. They have one of the most powerful armies in South America, supported by Russia and China. Maduro does not care that the people die of hunger; he is only concerned with paying a good salary for his soldiers and military officers; it is said that in Venezuela, a teacher has a salary of 30 dollars a month, while an army lieutenant has a monthly salary of 2000 dollars.

Denouncing Maduro's crimes is the only way we Venezuelans have to maintain hope that there will be a change. That is the reason why I have written this book and others. In particular, this book is the focus of my denunciations of the assaults on the press, our office, parliament, and the persecution of Freemasons.

At work, I dedicated time to the persecution of Freemasons because these events tried to be covered up and played against my reputation. I have recorded, demonstrated, and published each event in the Santiago Mariño Lodge Number 208 and the Grand Lodge in the media, setting legal precedents to initiate investigations.

I have been gradually insisting on the need to denounce Maduro before international bodies. I can mention some of the opinion articles that directly address the cases of persecution of Freemasons in Venezuela, which have been published in the newspaper El Nacional and also in my book "Maduro, the dictator of Venezuela. Crimes against humanity and more: Complaints of human rights violations, published in my opinion column", which can be purchased on Amazon, then I share the list of some of my referential posts:

Public letter to prosecutor Karim Khan, Oscar Pérez case and Freemasonry. By Esteban Oria - January 20, 2022, El Nacional https://www.elnacional.com/opinion/carta-publica-al-fiscal-karim-khan-caso-oscar-perez-y-la-masoneria/

William Jiménez identifies suspects in the former prosecutor's report delivered to the ICC. By Esteban Oria - July 21, 2022 https://www.elnacional.com/opinion/william-jimenez-identifica-sospechosos-en-informe-de-la-exfiscal-entregado-a-la-corte-penal-internacional/

Former investigator of the Grand Lodge denounces Maduro for the disappearance of Masons. By Esteban Oria - July 28, 2022, El Nacional https://www.elnacional.com/opinion/exinvestigador-de-la-gran-logia-denuncia-a-maduro-por-desaparicion-de-masones/

International Masonic Commission on Human Rights denounces the Maduro regime for crimes against Masons. By Esteban Oria-April 29, 2021, El Nacional. https://www.elnacional.com/opinion/comision-masonica-internacional-de-derechos-humanos-denuncia-al-regimen-de-maduro-por-crimenes-contra-masones/

They denounce Maduro for persecution and crimes against Venezuelan Masons. By Esteban Oria - February 18, 2021, El Nacional https://www.elnacional.com/opinion/denuncian-a-maduro-por-persecucion-y-crimenes-contra-masones-venezolanos/

France grants political asylum to a Freemason who frequented the Oscar Pérez lodge. By Esteban Oria - June 10, 2021, El Nacional https://www.elnacional.com/opinion/francia-otorga-asilo-politico-a-mason-que-frecuentaba-la-logia-de-oscar-perez/

Journey to the heart of hell: Nuria Ramos reveals the truth. By Esteban Oria - June 16, 2022 https://www.elnacional.com/opinion/viaje-al-corazon-del-infierno-nuria-ramos-devela-la-verdad/

Demonstrating Maduro's crimes against Freemasons has forced a group of Freemasons to form an informal Ad Hoc group under the name of the International Masonic Commission on Human Rights, which is created by the Venezuelan Federation of Political Scientists, an organization that I preside, with them to disclose all the crimes and persecutions that Maduro did and does against Masons.

We have written letters to the Prosecutor of the International Criminal Court, Karim Khan requesting him to continue the investigations into the crimes committed against the brothers Oscar Pérez and Diaz Pimentel and the rest of their companions; now we want to incorporate new investigations into the forced disappearances of the freemasons Wilmer Muñoz and Juan Hurtado. Regarding this letter, it is essential to highlight that we received a response from the ICC prosecutor's office. As received, we are waiting for more news.

Finally, I hope this book clarifies the reality that we Venezuelans live in and, the circumstances surrounding the country, how the Maduro dictatorship is expressed. The book invites us to reflect on the importance of maintaining firm convictions; in the case of Freemasons, it highlights the importance of honoring and asserting human rights, of our inalienable respect for public liberties, and in particular, honoring those who have contributed with the freedom of their nations.

Presidente de Venezuela Raúl Leoni

Before closing this writing, I want to celebrate the legacy left by illustrious Freemasons, generally in Venezuela reference has been made to Simón Bolívar, Miranda and other fathers of the country in the military field, but I want to exalt the work of another type of Freemason, they are leaders in the civil and scientific field, I want to praise the figure of Diego Bautista Urbaneja, president of Venezuela in 1947, Graduate in civil law, also José María Vargas, surgeon, scientist, professor and president 1835-1839 , also the figures of the fathers of Venezuelan liberal democracy Luis Beltran Prieto Secretary of the Government Junta of Venezuela in 1948 and President of the Congress of the Republic of Venezuela, Andrés Eloy Blanco president of the National Constituent Assembly called for the reform of the constitution in 1946 that establishes universal, direct and secret suffrage, Valmore Rodríguez Minister of Interior Relations of Venezuela 1945, Raúl Leoni Presid entity of the Republic of Venezuela in 1964, and make a special mention of Freemasons of the modern era who have stood out, it is about Jaime Lusinchi President of the Republic of Venezuela 1984, Octavio Lepage Interim President of Venezuela 1993 and

Juan Guaido President in Charge of the Bolivarian Republic of Venezuela 2019.

I hope that soon, our beloved Venezuela recovers its freedom; it depends to a great extent on the work that all Venezuelans do, contributing our grain of sand in this fight for our country's freedom. I hope this book helps raise awareness of the importance of granting protection to Venezuelans fleeing the horror of Maduro, each one of us has a story full of pain, but we stand upright, denouncing the crimes committed by the Maduro regime in the certainty that the international community hears us.

Maduro is a system made up of thousands of corrupt officials; each one of them owes a debt to international justice, and in each complaint we make, we expose them so that a fence of sanctions is created, and they are prevented from advancing in their outrages, the regime as such it is a criminal system that generates crimes against humanity, and therefore they deserve to be sitting before the International Criminal Court in The Hague answering to the judges.

EPILOGUE

I keep pleasant memories of Venezuela; I remember it was a country full of joy and love, despite our differences; as a people, we always kept our smiles.

We were blessed by God, who filled us with natural beauties, rivers with transparent waters, mountains and cloud forests, incredible fauna, and flora, parts of the Amazon, ancient tepuis, boundless plains, high-quality arable land, coasts with the most paradisiacal beaches ever seen, God also gave us immense oil deposits, gigantic mountains of iron and minerals, diamonds, gold mines of priceless value.

During the era of democracy in Venezuela, a period from 1958 to 1999, governments built immense public works, including the Guri dam, the bridge over Lake Maracaibo, the Central Park Towers, high-quality hospitals and majesty like Pérez Carreño, Jose María Vargas, El Llanito and its corresponding public financing, democracy made extensive highways and metro systems, modern buildings, excellent museums such as Sofia Imber and hundreds more in large and small cities, we had financing of public universities, private investment, full of jobs throughout the country, in Venezuela we received millions of emigrants from all over the world, many settled with their families and also made a fortune, it was the country of opportunities, it is It is true that the governments of democracy could not deal with corruption and the redistribution of wealth and this resulted in It was a deep inequality, poverty belts were established around the big cities, it was a crop of misery that we ended up paying for with the arrival of the populist Hugo Chávez, who came to power thanks to the vote of the poor, he offered economic freedom and defense of human rights, but he did the opposite, slowly and progressively exterminated our democracy and imposed his unipersonal model based on personalism and authoritarianism, they called it 21st Century Socialism, his ideal was to make a new idea of the old, rusty, unfortunate and hated socialism , I try by repeating precisely the same old socialism, what he did was implement a set of expropriation measures, in this way he expropriated thousands of companies, destroying thousands of jobs, his model was a vulgar copy of state capitalism of the Soviet economies, with the variant that the military occupied the addresses of the expropriated companies, thus creating a social base of privileges for the military, gradually the country became a kind of supervised democracy, where Chávez controlled all the powers of the state, from the parliament, the courts and the electoral system.

Chávez made the oil wealth his spoils of war; more than a trillion dollars entered the country for oil. However, this money has never been audited; even former Chavista ministers Hector Navarro and Jorge Giordani have denounced the loss of more than 300 billion dollars, all of it has been taken by corruption through the exchange system they established, where they favored companies to which they granted preferential dollars to import products that never arrived or that arrived with premiums that sometimes multiplied up to 30 times its face value.

What Chávez did was steal and loot the national public treasury; he did not do any relevant work during his term; on the contrary, he destroyed the health system and most of the schemes administered by the state; he introduced alliances with actors of dubious reputation, He did it with his friendship with Fidel Castro, who lent him thousands of intelligence and counterintelligence officials disguised as Cuban doctors to help him control the democratic opposition, but Chávez also made alliances with the Russians and acquired their highly sophisticated military weapons, that way. In the same way that Venezuela obtained both air and land superiority in the region, Chávez received Sukoy 30 planes from the Russians, Mil mi 24 helicopters, S 300 systems, hundreds of T 72 tanks, all kinds of missiles, millions of rifles, hundreds of combat batteries, in exchange for giving them unlimited access to state wealth, today the Russians control the leading oil and gold deposits, non-conforming, they Indebted to China worth billions of dollars to finance its social programs, which never worked and which were a front to steal money from the public treasury, it was in this way that Venezuela came to occupy the first positions in corruption in the world.

Chávez also armed militants from his party, the PSUV, arguing that he did it to defend his revolution. These groups were initially called Bolivarian circles. Later they would be called collectives; they were made up of criminals, and they controlled the neighborhoods through violence popular; it was in this way that they silenced the protests in the communities, then these groups took charge of other criminal activities such as kidnapping, extortion and drugs, it was in this way that Venezuela also came to locate three of its cities, among the most violent in the world, according to the Citizens' Council for Public Security and Criminal Justice. This think tank seeks to build consensus for solutions that improve security. They have drawn up a list of the 20 most dangerous cities in the world and have placed Caracas as the third most dangerous city in the world, all of this is the creation of the government of the late Chávez, and then Maduro arrives as his successor to secure the destruction from the country.

Maduro won the elections due to electoral fraud by a mere 200,000 votes difference from his challenger Capriles Radonski. Once in power, Maduro did was radicalized the Chávez regime, and he ended up handing over control to the military and also to the Cubans, now Maduro has increased the rates of violence to the extreme, so much so that during his mandates, he has quintupled the deaths and arrests of opponents. More than 250 deaths of protesters have been recorded during the protests throughout his term from 2014 to 2019; Maduro is responsible for the deaths of opponents under arrest, and he is denounced for state crimes against dissidents for extrajudicial executions; there are so many criminal cases that are accused that human rights organizations attached to the UN have endorsed more than 2000 forced disappearances.

At this point, Maduro and his officials are accused before the International Criminal Court, waiting to be called to testify before the thousands of requests filed by the victims, relatives, and witnesses. Maduro is a regime sanctioned by the international community, which has had countless state assets confiscated; he is also responsible for expelling more than 7 million immigrants who have left Venezuela in search of a safe place.

That Maduro has managed to destroy the basis of democracy by subduing all political structures, he has bribed opponents, getting them to accept his conditions to the detriment of the majority that seeks democracy. It has created a system of generating hunger through the induction of scarcity of essential products, including gasoline, with the idea of controlling the population through food cards; they call it CLAP bag, which is a box that includes food that is only given to members of his party and those who in his opinion behave well with the regime. Regarding medicines, in Venezuela, there are no medical supplies, and most doctors have emigrated to escape the dictatorship; only doctors graduated from Maduro schools with inadequate academic training, putting their lives at risk to the patients. In Venezuela, thousands of patients die at home because they cannot find a hospital bed.

This is the reality of Venezuelans, misery, poverty, and state terror. It is about informing the world that the Maduro regime does not and will not change; it continues to dominate in Venezuela with the same traits of human rights violations that characterize it. I think that the ideal solution continues to be free and transparent elections, but this is something that will be achieved if the international community maintains the system of sanctions and even increases them; they have to punish not only the perpetrators and masterminds of crimes of against humanity and corruption but also to the network of collaborators and beneficiaries.

For all this and more, Venezuelans have emigrated from our country in search of security and peace. In my book, a part of my story is embodied with the idea of making our reality visible. I have narrated the events I have witnessed related to my exile, with the idea of contributing to the search for justice for the victims I met in the framework of the hunt Maduro carried out against Masons both from my lodge and from others. Lodges, I firmly believe that the international justice system based on the conventions on human rights in the UN will channel in favor of Venezuelans, the procedures related to the causes in favor of the defense of human rights.

I lived the events narrated in the first person, and I have also published the stories of witnesses. Much of this material has already been published in my opinion column in the prestigious newspaper El Nacional, but the truth is that my story is one of the thousands that have the Venezuelans; It is a cry for help so that the world can listen and help us. We are facing a cruel dictatorship; what remains for us is to spread the truth about our reality in Venezuela; our goal is to raise awareness in the world in favor of helping Venezuela and Venezuelans, who are defenseless before a criminal system that governs our country controlling everything.

Next, I copy a brief sample of data corresponding to both the violations of the right to protest and freedom of conscience, freedom of expression, and economic freedom; that way, you will have an idea of the magnitude of the damage that Maduro and his regime have produced in Venezuela.

DATA VIOLATIONS OF ECONOMIC FREEDOMS EXPROPRIATIONS MADE IN VENEZUELA

CONSIGNED HOMES	LAND	5% of confiscations were paid
179 private buildings	838 farms	95% of takeovers were stolen
64 parking spaces	47 estates	62% of appropriations were abandoned
43 paralyzed urban complexes	Total 3.6 million hectares	12% of takeovers were resold to private companies
523,000 apartments and houses indirect expropriation (eviction ban)		Damage repair $433,000,000,000

MENTION OF SOME EXPROPRIATED COMPANIES

Hotel Hilton CARACAS	SIDETUR	Cargill
HIPERMERCADOS EXITO	Electricidad de Caracas	SENECA
Hotel Hilton Margarita	OWENS ILLINOIS	LACTEOS LOS ANDES
Sambil	Daka	Exxon Mobil
Conoco Phillips	SIDOR	CEMENTOS DE VENEZUELA
BANCO DE VENEZUELA	CONFERRY	CANTV
CATIVEN	PIGAP II	VENPRECAR
MATESI	COMSIGUA	ORINOCO IRON
COCA COLA FEMSA	AEROPOSTAL	60 EMPRESAS PETROLERAS
SMURFIT KAPPA	Puerto de Maracaibo	Puerto de Puerto Cabello

WHEN FLEEING VENEZUELA BECOMES A QUESTION OF LIFE OR DEATH

CEMEX	LAS CRISTINAS MINAS DE ORO	CRYSTALLEX
EMPRESAS	LAFARGE	HOLCIM
SUPERMERCADOS CADA	GALPONES DE EMPRESAS POLAR	MONACA-GRUMA
ENVASES INTERNACIONAL	AVENTUY	Industria Nacional de Artículos de Ferretería
Helmerich & Payne	AGROISLEÑA	VENOCO
SIDETUR	SIVENSA	Centrales azucareros
Planta de arroz CARGILL	Industria DIANA	Palmaven
Fertilizantes Nitrogenados de Oriente, SA	Fertilizantes Nitrogenados de Oriente, CEC	Fertilizantes Nitrogenados de Venezuela, SRL
Fertilizantes Nitrogenados de Venezuela, CEC (Fertinitro)	Gambrinus Corporation	Complejos hoteleros
Fabricas de vidrio	Compañías de lubricantes	Fábricas de envases de aluminio
Yacimientos de GAS	Yacimientos de Petróleo	Total 1087 Empresas
Cadenas alimentarias	Planta de taladros petroleros	Yacimientos de ORO
Fábricas de cartón	Fábricas de materiales de construcción	Supermercados

DATA VIOLATIONS FREEDOM OF THE PRESS
TELEVISIONS TAKEN

TVes	Venezolana de Televisión	Vive
123TV	Colombeia	TV ConCiencia
ANTV	TV FANB	Avila TV

PDVSA TV	Alba TV	TeleSUR
Showven	TVPEtare	

TELEVISIONS CLOSED

RCTV	PUMA TV	Canal de Noticias
Buena televisión	Telecaribe	ULA TV

INTERNATIONAL TELEVISION STATIONS BLOCKED

CNN EN ESPAÑOL	CARACOL	RCN
VPITV	TODONOTICIAS	TV CHILE
TVAZTECA	EL TIEMPO	ANTENA 3
INFOBAE	24 HORAS	NATIONAL GEOGRAPHICS
VH1 HD	CNN INTERNATIONAL	BBC WORLD
DW ESPAÑOL	TELEARUBA	TELECURACAO

CLOSED NEWSPAPERS AND THOSE THAT STOPPED CIRCULATION

EL NACIONAL	PANORAMA	Correo del Orinoco
Diario 2001	Diario VEA	El Mundo Economía y Negocios
El Nuevo País	Meridiano	Noticias al dia Notipascua
El Universal	Tal Cual	Ultimas Notas
Líder en Deportes	Anzoátegui	Antorcha
El Faro del Morro	El Mercurio Web	El Norte
El Tiempo	Metropolitano	Quinto Día

Mundo Oriental	Hora Cero	Nueva Prensa de Oriente
Apure	Visión Apureña	Diario Senderos De Apure Aragua
Ciudad Maracay	El Aragüeño	El Clarín
El Periodiquito	El Siglo	Barinas
De Frente	La Prensa de Barinas	El Diario de Los Llanos
La Noticia de Barinas	Bolívar	Correo del Caroní
El Diario de Guayana	El Expreso	El Luchdor
El Progreso	Nueva Prensa de Guayana	Primicia
Carabobo	Ciudad VLC	Diario LaCalle
Diario La Costa	El Carabobeño	Notitarde
Notitarde La Costa	Cojedes	Ciudad Cojedes
Las Noticias de Cojedes	Delta Amacuro	Notidiario
Distrito Capital	Ciudad CCS	Falcón
El Falconiano	La Mañana	Médano
Nuevo Día	Guárico	EL NACIONALISTA
El Tubazo Digital	Lara	El Impulso
El Informador	La Prensa	El Caroreño
El Diario de Lara	Mérida	Diario Frontera
Diario de Los Andes	Pico Bolívar	Miranda
Ciudad Petare	La Región	La Voz
Noticias del Tuy	Monagas	Ciudad Maturín
El Oriental	El Periódico de Monagas	El Sol de Maturín

La Prensa de Monagas	La Verdad de Monagas	Nueva Esparta
Diario Caribazo	El Sol de Margarita	La Hora
Portuguesa	El Regional	Última Hora
Noticiero Digital	Sucre	Región
Táchira	Diario Católico	Diario de Los Andes
Diario La Nación	Trujillo	El Tiempo
Diario de Los Andes	Yaracuy	Yaracuy al día
La Mosca	Zulia	El Regionl del Zulia
La Verdad	Versión Final	Notimedia
Semanario	6.º Poder	La Razón
Las Verdades de Miguel		

DATA VIOLATIONS FREEDOM OF CONSCIENCE
CIVILIAN POLITICAL PRISONERS

Carlos Alberto Jaimes Gomez	Gabriel Blanco	Tomeu Vadell
Juan Carlos Guillen Rosales	Reynaldo Cortez	Heath Mattew Jhon
Alcides Bracho	Alirio Zambrano	Leonvardo Antonio Primera Gutierrez
Alonso Meléndez	Jorge Toledo	Asterio José González
Emilio Negrin	José Luis Zambrano	Maria Auxiliadora Delgado Tabosky
Fernando Javier Betancourt	Carlos Germán Debiais García	Dirimo Antonio Pernía Bastidas
José Ángel Pereira Ruimwyk	Marco Antonio Garcés Carapaica	Dicxon Javier Giménez Giménez

WHEN FLEEING VENEZUELA BECOMES A QUESTION OF LIFE OR DEATH

Ivonne Coromoto Barrios Finol	Andry Ramón Finol	Larry Enrique Briceño Hinestroza
Daeven Enrique Rodríguez Argueta	Guillermo Jose Zarraga Lázaro	Juan Ubencio Machado
Robert Antonio Salas Moreno	Víctor Joel Cisneros	Roland Oswaldo Carreño Gutierrez
Frank Williams Cabaña Aldana	Luis Eduardo Mariño	Brayan Oropeza
Giuliani Espinoza	José Rodriguez Sevilla	Wilder Anderson Vásquez Velasquez
Gabriel Barros Romero	Jorge Enrique Alayeto Bigott	José Miguel Estrada González
Hugo Enrique Marino Salas	Aidaliz Guarisma	Yanin Fabiana Pernia Coronel
Juan Carlos Requesens Martinez	Ángela Lisbeth Exposito Carillo	Erasmo José Bolívar
Henryberth Rivas	Oswaldo Gabriel Castillo Lunar	Jesus Antonio Castro Gomez
Alberto José Bracho Rozquez	Argenis Gabriel Valera Ruiz	Deivis Miguel Malave Ruiz
Yolmer José Escalona Torrealba	Emirlendris Carolina Benitez	Marcos de Jesus Fuentes Gonzalez
José Eloy Rivas Díaz	Estela Carolina Ortega Velásquez	Luis Gerardo Salazar Marcano
Héctor José Rovain	Luis Enrique Molina Cerrada	Juan Bautista Guevara
Alexis Rafael Jimenez Jimenez	Cesar David Mayora Guacare	Antonio José Garbi Gonzalez
José Miguel Yeguez	Luis Eduardo Lira	Edgar José Barreto Sotillo
Juan Carlos Macualo Orozco		Jose Agustin Rondon Peers

Sixto José Salamanca Jimenez	Juan Carlos Ochoa Prieto	Yoslen José Broadbelt Mattey
Otoniel Guevara	Rolando Guevara	Rigoberto Moreno Carmona
Daniel Jesús Martínez Maneiro	Edgar Orlando Verdi Verdi	John Jairo Gasparini Ferbans
Esnel José Perales	Henry José Brito Marcano	Alejandro Rodriguez
Juan José Gámez Maza	Moisés Daniel González San Millán	Cosme Rafael Alcalá Acosta
Argenis Enrique Ugueto Benitez	Julio Cesar Sanchez Arias	Estewin Rojas Tapia
Robert José Franco Valera	Dario Estrada Peroz	Gilbert Barillas Fernandez
Luis Miguel Albornoz Rondon	Leovany José Alvarado Paz	Jesus Rafael Ramos Lopez
Carla Da Silva	Cesar Junior Altamar sarmiento	Juan José Torres Ramirez
Darwin Estibeen Herde Andrades	Douglas Javier Contreras Arellano	Yerferson Fernando Díaz Vásquez
Fernando Andres Noya Contramaestre	Franklin Duran	Ana María Pernia
Gustavo Adolfo Hernández Barranco	Jefferson Fernando Díaz Vasquez	Rodolfo Jesús Rodriguez Orellana
Jose Alberto Socorro Fernández	Josnars Adolfo Baduel Oyoque	Maryfrancy Marcano
Karen Hernández Rodriguez	Víctor Alexis Vásquez Contreras	Darwin Estibeen Herde Andrades
Jesus Rafael Ramos Lopez	Gerardo Cotichia	Francisco José Marcano Benavides
Oscar Leonardo Aguillon Garces	Rosmel Edecio Méndez Morales	Ysay Garcia Escobar

WHEN FLEEING VENEZUELA BECOMES A QUESTION OF LIFE OR DEATH

Enderson Rios Marin	José Armando Alvarado Flores	Roberto Bracho Coy
Angelo Moisés Rosales Santos	Leonardo David Chirinos Parra	Henry Anthony Sánchez Mora
Orlando Alberto Laufer Hernández	Jhon Hader Betancourt Restrepo	Orlando Enrique Chacin Castillo
Juan Francisco Antonio Mendoza	Royderman Machado Ramirez	César Horacio Belfort Rojas
Carlos Torrealba	Henry José Castillo Guevara	Luis Eduardo Villarroel Caña
José Valladares	Adolfo Torres Vargas	Víctor José Farías Quijada
Eulogio Del Pino	Gustavo José Malave Bucce	Martin Eduardo Álvarez García
Javier Tarazona	Carlos Alejandro Pérez Farías	José Ramón Cruz Marcano
Daniel Enrique Aguilera Gutiérrez	Enrique Naurix Parada	

MILITARY POLITICAL PRISONERS

Pedro Daniel Peñaloza Madrid	Feidy Rafael Montero	Jairo Eli Villegas Moreno
Alejandro Pérez Gámez	Héctor Armando Hernandez Da Costa	Ruben Augusto Bermudez Oviedo
Noe Ricardo Romero Lugo	Juan Francisco Diaz Castillo	Yecson Enrique Lozada Matute
Javier Rafael Peña	Ángel Vivas Perdomo	Victor Ignacio Rodríguez Romero
Luis Alberto Peña Arteaga	Luis Alexander Bandres Figueroa	Luis Alfredo Milanés Chirinos
Luis Heraldo Oviedo Piña	Nomar Salcedo Méndez	Roberto Catalino Romero Pérez

Juan Carlos Peña Palmienteri	Víctor Eduardo Soto Mendez	José de Jesus Gámez Bustamante
Abraham Américo Suárez Ramos	Adrian Leonardo De Gouveia De Sousa	Carlos Gustavo Macsotay Rauseo
Hevert David Glod Vásquez	Antonio Julio Scola Lugo	Edicxon Darwin Morillo Mujica
Andrés Alfonzo Paredes Soler	Asdrubal Gabriel Chirino Lopez	Geomer Narciso Martínez Natera
Edgar Jeús Díaz Vivenes	Carlos Enrique Rivero Martínez	Elias Jose
Kevin Manuel Charles Ramírez	Alberto José Polo Díaz	Darwin Antonio Solis Benitez
Jhite Thubal Hernández Palma	José Daniel González Ospedales	José Enrique Rico Arrieta
Hugo Alexander Carrillo Santana	Wolfan González Carrasco	Yeicer Moises Montero Mujica
Ronaldo Romero Aguinagalde	Yordanys Alirio Camacaro González	Alexis Bustamante Molano
Yofre Javier Castro Alviarez	Robert José Jiménez Ladera	Diana Daniela Diaz Cárdenas
Alfredo Saba Peña Diaz	Gustavo Enrique Carrero Angarita	Juan Pablo Saavedra Mejias
Miguel Rodriguez Torres	Luis Humberto De La Sotta Quiroga	Ricardo Efraín Gonzalez Torres
Juan Francisco Rodriguez Dos Ramos	Larry Osorio Chía	Alberto José Piñango Salas
Carla Yancelys Antón Farias	Hugo Rainer Aparicio Cabeza	Johan José González
Yurimar del Valle Rangel González	Yusimar Elisneth Montilla Ortega	Juan Carlos Marruffo Capozzi
Alvaro Martín Mestra Vallenilla	Deivis Esteban Mota Marrero	Igbert Jose Marin Chaparro

WHEN FLEEING VENEZUELA BECOMES A QUESTION OF LIFE OR DEATH

Juan Carlos Monasterios Vanegas	Pedro Javier Zambrano Hernandez	Darwin Andreizo Urdaneta Pardo
Ruperto Molina Ramirez	Franklin Alfredo Caldera Martinez	Jonathan Gabriel Rangel Rey
Nelson Enrique Santiago Valecillos	Alberto José Salazar Cabañas	Johnny Mejias Laya
José Rommel Acevedo Montañez	Oswaldo Valentín García Palomo	Ovidio Andres Carrasco Mosqueda
Cristian Gregorio Estrada Estrada	Eduardo Henriquez Pernía	Jefferson Gabriel Garcia Dos Ramos
Oswaldo Jose Gutierrez Guevara	Pedro Luis Garrido Guillen	Airan Seth Berry
Juan Carlos Caguaripano Scott	Alexander Jose Chávez Mogollon	Angel Orlando Perdomo Urtado
Carlos Enrique Conde Marquez	Anthony José Reyes	Cesar Eliant
Carlos Rosario	Damian Mora	Eduardo Jose Pérez Amaya
Ederson Roberto Rumi Mogollón	Dimas Omar Murillo Rubio	Luis Alfredo Lobo Medina
Estewin Andres Rojas Tapia	Erickson Alexander Chaya Barroeta	Evan Antonio Rincón Piñeiro
Gustavo Enrique Alvarez Granadillo	Francisco Luna	Franklin Antonio Leal Mendoza
Jackson Leiner Taquiva Becerra	Jeremy Jesús González Lopez	Jesus Alberto Colmenares Gallardo
Jesus Manuel Ramos López	Jesús Manuel Ramos López	Jonathan Rafael Franco Quiñonez
José Alberto Trejo Castillo	Jose Alexander Sanquino Escalante	Jose Angel Barreno Cordonez

Jose Antonio Moreno Peñaloza	José Ibienay Ruiz Delgado	José Manuel Mendoza González
José Rafael Blanco Volcán	Juan Fredd Jesús Acosta Ysea	Junior de Jesús Silva Herrera
Junior Ojeda	Leandro Leomar Chirinos Parra	Leonard Briceño
Leonardo Carrillo Primera	Luis Manuel Paiva Soto	Luxe Alexander Denman
Miguel Angel Plaza Mendez	Rafael Enrique Castro Sandoval	Samaira del Valle Romero Armario
Rawuy José Rosales Faria	Renny Adelso Olivares Moreno	Raúl Eduardo Manzanilla Almao
Richard Rafael Alemán Castellano	Ricardo David Fonseca Mosquera	Roberto Andres Rondon Restrepo
Tony Guevara	Victor Daniel Parra	Victor Perozo
Wilmer Oswaldo Salinas Sánchez	Juan Luis Gutierrez Aranguren	Angel Barrios Fuenmayor
Eddie José Valladares Cáceres	Hebert Alfonso Cambero Sequera	Hector Jesus Coronel
Jefferson Jhosue Diaz Mendoza	Nelson Miguel Zabaleta Fernandez	Andrés Ramón Thomson Martinez
Nery Adolfo Cordova Moreno	Victor José Ascanio Castillo	Adelis Pastor Rosales Peroza
Anderson Daniel Farnetano Yamboos	Carlos Eduardo Leon Nuñes	Ervin José Gragirena Echzuría
Ervin José Gragirena Echzuría	Jose Gregorio Pavon Medina	Juan Carlos Bolívar Rodríguez
Miguel Ambrosio Palacio Salcedo	Miguel José Salazar Polanco	Oneiver José Paredes

Rafael Antonio Villafranca López	Rubén Darío Fernández Figueroa	Ramón Ali Peñalver Vasquez
Hebert Andrés Amaron Quintero	Carlos Alfonso Parra Perez	Durvis Enrique Melean Vargas
Juan Carlos Ramos	Miguel Alberto Castillo Cedeño	Miguel Carmelo Sisco Mora
Carlos Eduardo Lozada Saavedra	Ramón Antonio Lozada Saavedra	Fredy Alberto Mogollon Rojas
Rafael Ernesto Díaz Cuello	Rafael Rocendo Rivero	Rigoberto Pinzón Palencia
Noriega Manrique		

KILLED IN THE PROTESTS AGAINST MADURO 2014

Bassil Da Costa	Juan Carlos Montoya	Robert Redman
José Ernesto Méndez	Génesis Carmona	Luzmila Petit de Colina
Julio Eduardo González Pinto	Delia Elena Lobo	Arturo Alexis Martínez
Elvis Rafael Durán De La Rosa	José Alejandro Márquez	Geraldine Moreno
Willmer Carballo Amaya	Jimmy Vargas	Antonio José Valbuena Morales
Joan Quintero	Giovanni Pantoja	Eduardo Anzola}
María Julieta Heredia	Luis Gutiérrez Camargo	José Gregorio Amaris Castillo
Deivis Durán Useche	Giselle Rubilar	Daniel Tinoco
Acner Isaac López Lyon	Ramzor Bracho	Guillermo Sánchez

Jesús Eduardo Acosta	Francisco Madrid	Anthony Rojas
José Guillén Araque	Wilfredo Rey	Argenis Hernández
Jhon Castillo	Jesús Labrador	Miguel Antonio Parra
Adriana Urquiola	Roberto Annese	Mariana Ceballos
Luis Alberto Romero Moncada	José Steven Colina	Josue Farías
José Daza		

KILLED IN THE PROTESTS AGAINST MADURO 2017

Brayan David Principal Giménez	Gruseny Antonio Calderón Scirpatempo	Carlos José Moreno
Paola Andreína Ramírez Gómez	Niumar José San Clemente Barrios	Mervin Fernando Guitian Díaz
Albert Alejandro Rodríguez Aponte	Ramón Ernesto Martínez Cegarra	Francisco Javier González Núñez
Jairo Ortiz	Daniel Alejandro Queliz Araca	Miguel Ángel Colmenárez Milano
Kelvin Steeven León	Jairo Ramírez	William Heriberto Marrero Rebolledo
Robert Joel Centeno Briceño	Jonathan Antonio Meneses López	Elio Manuel Pacheco Pérez
Romer Stivenson Zamora	Yorgeiber Rafael Barrena Bolívar	Kenyer Alexander Aranguren Pérez
Manuel Pérez	Natalie Martínez	José Ramón Gutiérrez
Ángel Lugo Salas	Estefany Tapias	Almelina Carrillo Virgüez
Renzo Rodríguez Rodas	Jesús Leonardo Sulbarán	Luis Alberto Márquez
Orlando Johan Jhosep Medina Aguilar	Christian Humberto Ochoa Soriano	Jackson Enrique Hernández Hernández

WHEN FLEEING VENEZUELA BECOMES A QUESTION OF LIFE OR DEATH

Juan Pablo Pernalete	Eyker Daniel Rojas Gil	Yonathan Eduardo Quintero Arenas
Carlos Eduardo Aranguren Salcedo	Ángel Enrique Moreira González	Ana Victoria Colmenárez de Hernández
María de los Ángeles Guanipa	Jesús Armando Alonso Valera	Armando Cañizales Carrillo
Daniel Gamboa	Jesús Asdrúbal Sarmiento	Luis Eloy Pacheco
Carlos Mora	Gerardo José Barrera Alonso	Hecder Vladimir Lugo Pérez
Miguel Medina	Luis José Alviarez Chacón	Anderson Enrique Dugarte Dugarte
Diego Armando Hernández Barón	Yeison Nathanael Mora Castillo	José Francisco Guerrero Contreras
Diego Fernando Arellano De Figueredo	Manuel Felipe Castellanos Molina	Freddy Jerson Ramírez Calderón
Reinaldo Márquez Rada	Paúl René Moreno Camacho	Daniel Rodríguez Quevedo
Jorge David Escandón Chiquito	Edy Alejandro Terán Aguilar	Yorman Ali Bervecia Cabeza
Jhon Alberto Quintero	Miguel Ángel Bravo Martínez	Alfredo José Briceño Carrizález
Ynigo Jesús Leiva	Freiber Pérez Vielma	Juan Antonio Sánchez Suárez
Erick Antonio Molina Contreras	Augusto Sergio Puga Velásquez	Adrián José Duque Bravo
Manuel Alejandro Sosa Aponte	Danny José Subero	César David Pereira Villegas
Nelson Antonio Moncada Gómez	María Estefanía Rodríguez	Luis Miguel Gutiérrez Molina
Yoinier Javier Peña Hernández	Sócrates Jesús Salgado Romero	José Amador Lorenzo González

JOSÉ ESTEBAN ORIA

Orlando Figuera	Neomar Lander	Luis Alberto Machado Valdez
Douglas Acevedo Sánchez Lamus	Luis Enrique Vera Sulbarán	Nelson Daniel Arévalo Avendaño
Alexander Rafael Sanoja Sánchez	José Gregorio Pérez Pérez	Fabián Urbina
David José Vallenilla Luis	Lendy José Guanipa Millán	Ronny Alberto Parra Araujo
Jhonatan José Zavatti Serrano	Javier Alexander Toro Trejo	Isael Jesús Macadán Aquino
Luiyin Alfonso Paz Borjas	Roberto Enrique Durán Ramírez	Eduardo José Márquez Albarrán
Víctor Manuel Betancourt	Alfredo José Figuera Gutiérrez	José Rodolfo Bouzamayor Bravo
Rubén Alexander Morillo Pereira	Fernando Rojas Rubio	José Gregorio Mendoza Durán
Ramsés Enrique Martínez	Engelberth Duque	Jonathan Alexander Giménez Vaamonde
Rubén Darío González Jiménez	Manuel Ángel Villalobos Urdaneta	Oswaldo Rafael Britt
Yanet Angulo Parra	Xiomara Soledad Scott	Héctor Alejandro Anuel Moreno
Ronney Eloy Tejera Soler	Eury Rafael Hurtado	Andrés José Uzcátegui Ávila
Jean Luis Camarillo Deluque	Víctor Manuel Márquez Luengo	Yamile Margarita Vásquez Gómez
Carlos Alberto Paredes Carrizo	Rafael Antonio Balza Vergara	Enderson Enrique Calderas Ramírez
Jean Carlos Aponte	Rafael Celestino Canache Guaina	Gilimber Terán
Leonardo Augusto González Barreto	José Miguel Pestano	José Gustavo Leal Villasmil

Eduardo Gil Rodríguez	Marcel Pereira	Albert Rosales
Wilmer Smith Flores Carrascal	Ender Rafael Peña Sepúlveda	Juan José Monges Páez
Oneiver Jhoan Quiñones Ramírez	Ronald Ramírez Rosales	Luis Eduardo Ortiz
Adrián Smith Rodríguez Sánchez	Ricardo Campos	Luis Beltrán Zambrano Lucena
Ángelo Yordano Méndez	Eduardo Olave	José Fernando Sánchez Sánchez
Haider Ocando	Hilario José Gutiérrez	Daniela de Jesús Salomón Machado
Antony Rodrigo Labrador	Jhonny Alfredo Colmenares Colmenárez	Ramón Antonio Rivas
Wilmerys Zerpa	Eduardo Orozco	Luis Guillermo Espinoza
Anyelo Rafael Quintero Rivas	Miguel Castillo Bracho	Elvis Andonis Montilla Pérez

KILLED IN THE PROTESTS AGAINST MADURO 2019

Alixon Osorio Dos Santos Pizani	Stefany Maholy Layoy Natera	Franklin Alexánder Figuera
Carlos Alfredo Olivares Bonalde	Cleiner José Romero	Luisdy Bolívar
Ángel Tovar	Yeimbert José Rangel	Yhonny Alejandro Hernández Ojeda
Edwar José Marrero	Gustavo Ramirez	Efrén Sandalio Castillo
Wilmer Mendoza	Ivan Antonio Alvarez Fernández	Juan Rafael Medina Torres
Luigi Guerreo Ovalles	Jhonny Jesus Pacheco Vega	Nick Samuel Borges
Yeskarly José Gil	Emmanuel Zambrano	Francisco Acosta

Andrés Rafael Rodríguez Oliveros	Pedro Díaz	Yohni José Godoy Buitrago
Rael Alabbi	Luis Alberto Martínez	Germán Cohen
Frank David Correa Gutierrez	Adán Pérez	Luis Francisco Perez
Robert Cabello	Daniel Véliz	Alfredo Núñez
Moisés Araujo	Kevin Antonio Cárdenas Blanquez	

WEB PAGES BLOCKED BY THE STATE + 1,000 WEBSITES

insightcrime.org	es.insightcrime.org	soundcloud.com
elnacional.com	albertonews.com	www.caraotadigital.net
caraotadigital.xyz	caraotadigital.news	lapatilla.com
hugocarvajal.com	venezuelazonagris.com	www.2001.com.ve
venezolanosenusa.net	telesurlibre.com	albertonews.com
www.caraotadigital.net	telesurlibre.com	caraotadigital.news
lapatilla.com	alnavio.com	www.aporrea.org
armando.info	dolartoday.com	dolartoday.info
dolartoday.org	bit.ly/venezuela911	efectococuyo.com
elpitazo.net	www.eltiempo.com	evtvmiami.com
diariolaregion.net	www.infobae.com	infodio.com
lamananadigital.com	maduradas.com	minuto30.com
monitoreamos.com	noticialdia.com	noticiaaldia.com
noticiasvenezuela.org	www.el-nacional.com	www.noticierodigital.com
www.ntn24.com	pvenezuela.com	presidenciave.com

puntodecorte.com	*reddit.com*	*runrun.es*
livestream.com	*sumarium.es*	*sunoticiero.com*
venezuelaaidlive.com	*www.venezuelaaldia.com*	*www.ventevenezuela.org*
vivoplay.net	*vpitv.com*	*zello.com*
Alekboyd.blogspot.co.uk	*Alekboyd.blogspot.com*	*Robertopatino.com*
www.vamosbien.com	*www.vcrisis.com*	*vdebate.blogspot.com*

201